YOUTH LEAGUE
BASEBALL

COACH'S EDITION

PROMOTING ATHLETICS · PHYSICAL EDUCATION · RECREATION

Athletic
Institute

SINCE 1934

THE ATHLETIC INSTITUTE

**Library of Congress
Catalog Card Number 74-21956
ISBN 87670-082-2**

Published by
THE ATHLETIC INSTITUTE
200 Castlewood Drive
North Palm Beach, FL 33408
U.S.A.

A Word From The Publisher

For some time the challenge has been raised, "Why do we have youth league programs?" Many have attempted to answer this highly complex question, yet we find little in the way of published material that affords solutions to the problem.

This coaches edition of Youth League Baseball may not be the answer to every problem facing youth league baseball programs, but we believe it does answer the question, "What is a volunteer manager?" and tells the role a manager should play in accepting this important responsibility.

The Athletic Institute is grateful to James H. Toner for his contributing essay "Coaching and Managing Youth League Baseball", also a special recognition to the team players and their coaches, who participate in this program.

Howard J. Bruns
President and Chief Executive Officer
The Athletic Institute

D. E. Bushore
Executive Director
The Athletic Institute

Acknowledgment

The Athletic Institute would like to acknowledge contributions of the following for their giving of knowledge and time to make this publication a resource tool for the volunteer coach.

Tom Easton
Palm Beach Gardens Youth Athletic Association
Palm Beach Gardens, Florida

Louis (Rags) Scheuermann
New Orleans Recreation Dept.
New Orleans, Louisiana

James H. Toner, Ph.D
Norwich University
Defensive Strategy Consultant

Appreciation too is extended to the team players who participated in this program.

Cover Photo
Lake Worth Mustangs All-Stars, Lake Worth, Florida

Contents

Basic strategy and tactics

Rules Simplified

Philosophy

**The Responsibility
of a Volunteer Coach**

**Care of
Athletic Injuries**

Coaching and Managing Youth League Baseball

Whatever you do, work at it with your whole being.
— Colossians 3:23 (NAB)

In his book **The Life That Ruth Built,** the late Marshall Smelser, an historian at the University of Notre Dame, reported that the Kansas City Royals' team psychologist, in the years 1970 to 1973, learned that only **one in fifteen hundred** male high school graduates had good enough eyes, speed, intelligence, and reaction time to make it worth the cost of trying to teach him to play professional baseball — at even the lowest minor-league level.[1] Only a handful of youth league baseball players, then, will ever don the uniform of a professional baseball team. If there are very few career opportunities for youth leaguers — and, of course, none for the volunteer managers and coaches who make the leagues operate — why bother with the effort?

One answer to that question has always been so that the kids can have fun. Almost everyone who has been involved for a while in youth-league sports will know coaches whose approach to athletics is simply to let the kids have fun. Not long ago I went to see two "all-star" youth-league baseball teams play a game. One team was taking batting practice and going through their usual pre-game warm-up routines. The kids on the other team were playing on swings and monkey bars. Now there is nothing wrong with youngsters playing on playground equipment; that is the reason the swings were installed in the first place. I think there is something wrong with the team's manager. His youngsters were supposedly preparing for an "all-star" youth league game. But their manager was unwilling to discipline them enough to keep their minds on the game. (I must confess that I am glad to report that the team that took the batting practice won the game!) Don't misunderstand me, please. I am not at all opposed to kids' having fun in playing youth league baseball; that is **one** — but only one — of the purposes of such baseball activity.

As a teacher, I like to think of my students having "fun" — even in a college classroom — learning. But I know that learning is very demanding work. Thomas Edison once said that genius is a blend of 99% perspiration and 1% inspiration. Whether a student is trying to learn calculus or trying to learn the technique of a baseball rundown play, he must learn to work at it. There are many variations on the story of why some athletes succeed in their sports, and others never get far beyond mediocrity. But one story puts it well: Some become successful because they **work** at playing while others only **play** at playing. The youth league coach should definitely want his kids to enjoy baseball — to have fun playing it. But the key is that the youngsters are learning baseball; they are not engaging in horse play, swinging on swings or monkey bars, or day-dreaming. Who would want his child's school teacher to ignore teaching subjects such as history, mathematics, spelling, and geography because the teacher wanted the students to "have fun"? If the youth leaguers have fun by playing baseball, fine; but the manager must remember that his purpose for having a team is to teach them baseball, not to let them run around in activities not related to their purpose for being in a youth league.

Another answer to the question of why kids should participate in youth-league baseball usually takes the form of recommendations about "competition" and "winning." "Show me a gracious loser," someone has said, "and I'll show you a loser." And everyone has heard the remark attributed to Vince Lombardi, the Green Bay Packers' former coach: "Winning isn't the most important thing; it's the only thing." There **is** something to this. Have you ever watched a team of kids who have just suffered their tenth consecutive loss? If the manager tries to tell them that all that matters is how they play the game, he may find that convincing them of that won't be very easy. There are not too many coaches, however, who are indifferent about winning; more prevalent is the coach who seems desperate to win, perhaps to re-live his own youth through the lives of his young athletes. (Why is it, by the way, that so many of these over-zealous coaches seem never to have excelled in a sport themselves in high school?)

Anyone who loves baseball, as I do, has seen (or, worse, played for) the parody of a youth league coach: a screaming tyrannical martinet whose power over a hapless group of little kids goes right to his head, converting him into a kind of athletic fascist whose principal goal in life is "winning." As a result of his single-minded commitment to victory, the coach may curse at umpires, insult his players after errors, refuse to play his less able athletes, and generally represent all that is contemptible about contemporary American sports. It's small wonder that many wise and decent people ridicule kids' sports when they see the megalomania of some adults who are supposed to be teaching the joy of a sport rather than its horror.

There is, however, another side to this question of "winning." About ten years ago, I read Charles Reich's **The Greening of America**. His contention was that the new American youth would forsake the "stupidity" of competition for the greener pastures of tender harmony, cooperation, and love feasting. A decade ago, I thought that was nonsense; I still do. Let me put it plainly: I believe deeply in the value of fair, honest, and reasonable competition — whether it involves free enterprise economics, spelling bees, college placement exams, or youth league baseball. I cannot for a moment agree with those who would ban kids' sports because "Johnny" struck out and thus has met with disappointment, defeat, or frustration. Still, I have known coaches who think that winning and losing are the same thing, and I have known coaches to whom all that matters is winning.

Well, a plague on both your houses! Coaches whose idea of kids' sports amounts to little more than victory are incompetent and should not be permitted to teach anything; but coaches who can discover no difference between winning and losing are equally unable to teach many of the things that a sports program should teach.

Winning **is** important. No baseball player or coach wants to listen to a fighting charge such as, "Get out there and lose one for the Gipper!" Competition can help foster both intellectual and physical skills; but just as there are laws governing the competition of adults in the business world, so there are rules governing children's games. If an adult lies, cheats, or steals in the business world, he will not long be tolerated among his honest colleagues. If a youth league coach exhibits conduct unbecoming a gentleman and a teacher — something coaches are supposed to be — he should not long be tolerated among his serious coaching colleagues. Whether we like it or not, our summer coaches serve as role-models for our children. As we would not (I hope) put up with insolence or incompetence in our children's classroom teachers, neither should we tolerate youth-league coaches who are bellicose tyrants or indifferent baseball ne'er-do-wells. The former manager of the Los Angeles Dodgers, Walter Alston, put it well: "In short, baseball needs more coaches who are good teachers."[2]

I have tried to answer the question about the value of youth-league baseball: It is part of a youngster's education. It is not just "fun-and-games," but is, rather, a serious enterprise — as is going to school or to church. We hope the youngster will have fun — but the fun comes through baseball, not despite it. We hope the youngster's team will win at least a few games, but "victory" is NOT what youth-league baseball is all about. The President of Oglethorpe University recently put it this way:

> A sports program offers important advantages to students: It develops physical strength, agility, and stamina; and it teaches qualities of leadership, teamwork, and self-discipline . . . Good sportsmanship should be emphasized. Civility, playing by the rules, and being a good loser and a graceful winner are important elements in the sports tradition and are essential if an athletic program is to have educational value.[3]

Who could say it better than Babe Ruth himself: "Play fair, win honestly, don't brag about winning or cry over losing."[4]

Five Rules of Coaching

I had a roommate in college who used to tell me that there is an exception to every rule — except that rule, to which there is no exception. Still, I would venture five "rules" of my own about kids' coaches. Not everyone will agree with them; and perhaps they're not too easy to live up to.

First, the coach must know baseball and enjoy it. He is, after all trying to coach someone about something. If he doesn't understand the basics of the game, he can't teach it; if he doesn't enjoy it, he won't want to teach it. This does not mean that the coach must be a former career athlete, or even a high school or college star. In fact, many professional athletes, although physically gifted, may be unable to communicate well with those less talented than themselves. And many excellent coaches may possess superior knowledge of the game by virtue of reading, study, and conversation about sport rather than from superior physical talents. (Look at many of today's major league managers.)

Second, the coach must know his youngsters and enjoy them. He is, after all, coaching to help the kids — and not for his personal ego gratification. The game is for the kids, not for coaches who wish they were Billy Martin. Once on the diamond, the coach can exhort and encourage; but he cannot play the game. If the youngsters whom he has taught cannot figure out how to respond to developing situations themselves, the coach's drills and situations (given elsewhere in this handbook) won't amount to much.

Third, the coach must serve as an example (that is, a good example). If a coach uses foul language, continually screams at players, cannot express himself in reasonable English, and generally gives the appearance of being the thirteenth member of the "Dirty Dozen," watch his team. They will, very probably, scream at each other or at umpires, use foul language, blather, and generally act as though they had become the delinquents which the joy and discipline of a sport can help prevent.

Fourth, the coach must teach, in addition to fundamental baseball skills and self-discipline, the art and science of effort. Kids will want to win, and I think that's all right — but not in any way and not at any price. What genuinely matters is that every youngster on the team should learn that if he or she gives the game the best effort possible — plus a shade more — then they have won, regardless of the score; they have beaten themselves. **Discipline** and **teamwork** and **sweat** — these are not evil words. That the coach should not be a screamer doesn't mean that he can't expect hard work and demand attention. His first goal is to get the most out of his team for the benefit of the individual players — not for the "honor and glory" of the coach. My view of this, as an amateur manager, is supported by Walter Alston, a most successful professional baseball manager:

> The league standing does not necessarily indicate how good or how bad a coach really is. If he has gotten 100 per cent from his men, maneuvering them skillfully, using proper defenses and changing pitchers when he should, he can feel he has done a most satisfactory job.[5]

Fifth, and finally, the manager should coach as he himself would wish to be coached. I suppose you could call that the "Golden Rule of Youth League Baseball Managing." At the end of every season, each coach should ask himself one question: "If I had been the least athletically talented player on my team, how would I have liked playing for me?" Did the youngster learn the fundamentals of the game? Did he grow morally, mentally, and physically? Did he become a little more self-assured? A little more honest about himself and his abilities? Did he enjoy and profit from the discipline, the logic, and the intelligence of baseball? Did he learn at least some of those great virtues that youth league literature always talks about? If so, one has to say, "Hey coach, thanks a lot!" That's all the coach needs to keep him warm all winter.

If all the above seems too "philosophical," I thought I would bring it a bit more down to earth in giving below the exact instructions which I give to my team (in a written handout) before the season starts. My team is named the Dodgers, but I have used similar instructions with other teams (and other levels of baseball):

Dodgers are expected to ask questions if they do not understand instructions, basic plays, or rules. Because I think of youth league baseball as **part of a youngster's education** — and not as preparation for playing high school, college, or pro baseball — I think youngsters can profit a great deal from learning that, when they don't understand something, they must ask questions. As manager, I do not insist upon flawless play (every kid will make errors and strike out); nor do I insist upon winning. I will insist upon attention and concentration. Dodgers will be neat and clean for games, with shirts tucked in and the uniform worn properly. Whatever Dodgers **think** they know about the game of baseball, they should learn that there's always more to know. No one — not even Billy Martin — knows it all. Dodgers are expected to try hard, but self-discipline demands that Dodgers not be boastful after winning or depressed after losing. We will practice all the basic plays, most of which are diagrammed in this manual (My twelve basic situations are also given in this Handbook), so that Dodgers will know what to do with the baseball when it comes to them. Dodgers will show respect for all people connected with our baseball league. If the kids or the parents disagree with these objectives, they should not be part of the Northfield (Vermont) Dodgers . . . The basic objective of youth league baseball is to help build character — courage, temperance, fairness, and knowledge; the goal is not just to win or to have fun.

Dodgers will not use language that is profane or abusive. Swearing will not be tolerated. Dodgers will be taught to play as a team, and to observe safety rules very strictly. Dodgers will be **on time** for practices, and I ask that the youngsters themselves call me if they cannot come to a parctice or game. No Dodger will ridicule, mock, or make fun of any other player. And no Dodger will be on our team if he will not be a good sport who plays hard, but fair, and follows the rules of the game. Good conduct — such as no spitting and no bad language — will be essential if the youngster wants to play for the Dodgers . . . These rules should be understood right from the beginning of the season.[6]

To help my team (and their parents) to remember all that, I have developed a simple mnemonic device, which keeps my performance rules in mind:

When in doubt, ask questions
Insist upon concentration and attention
Neatness counts
Never be fully satisfied with knowledge and execution of baseball skills
Emphasize self-discipline
Remember the basic plays and situations
Show respect for managers, coaches, umpires, other players, and fans

The rest of the memory aid is this:

Language that's profane or obscene
Only care about themselves
Safety doesn't count
Evade responsibility
Ridicule, mock, or make fun of players
Show contempt for rules, fair play, and sportsmanship.

I instruct my team that, of course, the first group of rules is for WINNERS; the LOSERS follow the second group. I include one paragraph in my handout which is directly aimed at the parents:

Please tell your Dodger that he is expected to try hard — we'll keep saying 125%. And he is expected to act properly on and off the field. BUT NO ONE WILL EVER YELL AT HIM FOR MAKING AN ERROR OR STRIKING OUT. He will be corrected when a mistake is made, but the correction will be made by the manager or coach in the same way that HE would like to be corrected if he had made the mistake.

I hope that all of you who use this Athletic Institute publication will enjoy and profit from it as you go about the two jobs of (1) teaching kids baseball, and (2) just plain teaching kids. In my judgment, they're just about the same thing. I end my own manual to my "Dodgers" this way:

I believe that there is much of value in youth baseball, if it is regarded not simply as "having fun" and not simply as "winning." We will have a lot of fun, and we will win — and lose (there's no shame in that at all). But the first job is this: "Train a boy in the way he should go; even when he is old, he will not swerve from it" (Proverbs, 22.6 [NAB]).

[1]Marshall Smelser, **The Life That Ruth Built** (New York: Quadrangle/The New York Times Book Co., 1975). pp. 408, 476.

[2]Walter Alston and Don Weiskopf, **The Baseball Handbook** (Boston: Allyn and Bacon, Inc., 1979), p. 310.

[3]Manning M. Pattillo, Jr., "Colleges Must Make Sure that Athetics Don't Hinder the Educational Process," **The Chronicle of Higher Education,** 21 October 1981, p. 25.

[4]Babe Ruth, as quoted in Alston and Weiskopf, **The Baseball Handbook,** p. 475.

[5]Alston and Weiskopf, **The Baseball Handbook,** p. 310.

[6]James H. Toner, "Northfield Dodgers Baseball Manual: A Guide for Coaches, Parents, and Players," mimeographed, 1981, pp. 4-5.

the responsibilities of a volunteer manager

Liability

Because they have volunteered their time, many volunteer managers never stop to think that they are responsible for the welfare of the youngsters they coach. The feeling is that since they are donating their time they are not really held responsible. *Nothing could be further from the truth.*

Morally, the volunteer manager is held responsible for the psychological damage he may cause youngsters. Parents want him to see that proper attitudes are instilled in their youngsters' minds. The physical aspect is also important. Volunteers who agree to coach also agree to be responsible for the safety of the young people they coach. If proven negligent, managers may be held liable for physical harm incurred by players in their charge.

Included in this section are areas about which a conscientious person will become informed before he begins working as a volunteer manager.

Safe Equipment

The old saying, "You get what you paid for," applies here — however, what you get, perhaps, are broken collar bones and sprained ankles when the equipment purchased is of poor quality.

Poor and Inadequate Facilities

Such facilities can result in a multitude of injuries. Examples are ruts and holes in the field of play and rocks on the infield of a ball diamond. All a good manager has to do is look around and say to himself, "Do things look safe?" If they do, he has no problems.

Drink Plenty of Liquids During Practice Sessions

Contrary to what a lot of old-timers think, water is not only good to give out during practice, it will help prevent heat exhaustion and dehydration.

There is absolutely no scientific evidence that withholding liquids from athletes during practice will make them stronger and tougher. Medical research indicates that during exercise it is necessary to replace water loss (perspiration) hour by hour.

Physical Examinations

All youngsters participating on the team should have a physical examination with written approval from a medical doctor stating they are physically fit to participate in athletic competition. DON'T TAKE THE CHANCE OF SERIOUS INJURY BECAUSE YOU DIDN'T TAKE THE TIME TO SEE WHETHER THE PLAYER WAS MEDICALLY FIT!

How Many Games to Play During the Season?

Many volunteer managers get wrapped up in the thrill of coaching (especially if it's a winning team), so much so that they go and schedule extra games for the kids. Besides being unrealistic, it is unhealthy for a youngster to be involved in too many games per season. Why? Here are a few reasons.

1. The strain of too many baseball games can drastically affect the overall system of a youngster during adolescence.

2. The psychological strain of winning and losing can take its toll on the emotional growth of a youngster.

3. Young people have home, school and social responsibilities which can be affected by overemphasis on the number of games played.

Know The Rules

Agreeing to coach means you also agree to know the rules. A coach who "thinks" he knows the rules because he watches television on weekends, is only fooling himself. There is a big difference between pro rules and high school or youth league rules. Many games have been lost simply because a coach did not take the time to learn the difference.

You owe it to your players and yourself to brush up. Here is where you can find the rules for your league.

Babe Ruth Baseball
P.O. Box 5000
1770 Brunswick Ave.
Trenton, NJ 08638

Little League Baseball Inc.
P.O. Box 3485
Williamsport, PA 17701

Pony Baseball, Inc.
P.O. Box 225
Washington, PA 15301

Conditioning

Exercise may be stressed. The younger person of today does not need the same amount of time that an adult needs to get prepared for a season of play. It is important though, to make sure the younger person is warmed up and ready to play.

Once the season begins you may also prepare team exercises or warmups to be used in preparation of your games. This is time well spent in making sure your players are ready to go.

Staying in shape may not seem important to the younger players. It is up to you as coach to give them advice and spend time in a team meeting on the subject.

Warm Up And
Avoid Injury

Care of Athletic Injuries

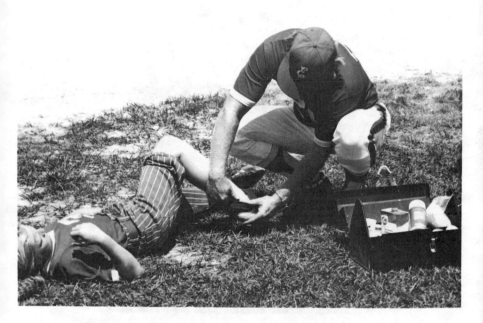

Did you ever stop to think that your actions in case of an injury could, in the most extreme case, save an individual's life or, in the mildest case, have your player back in action in a matter of minutes? Think about it — it's true.

The care of athletic injuries is a subject too vast and complicated to cover in total. However, our purpose in this publication is to inform you, the volunteer coach, as to the (1) practical equipment you should have on hand at all times, (2) the most common injuries and (3) the immediate first-aid steps to follow in case of one of these injuries.

Included in this section are areas about which a conscientious person will become informed before he begins working as a volunteer coach.

Practical Needs

1. Most sporting goods stores carry regular coach's first-aid kits. As a check list, however, all coach's first-aid kits should contain:

- Adhesive tape — several different sizes for several purposes.
- Ammonia caps for dizziness
- Antiseptic solution (betadine)
- Aspirin for simple headaches
- Plastic bottles for carrying water
- Cold packs
- Elastic wraps of various sizes
- Gauze pads
- Soap
- Salt tablets for hot humid weather
- Scissors
- Tongue depressors
- Eyewash solution with eyewash glass
- Small flashlight (pen size)

Emergencies

The telephone number of the nearest ambulance service should be taped inside the first-aid kit. Always know where the closest available phone is at every game or practice site. Also tape the proper amount of change to the inside of the first-aid kit, in case the closest phone is a pay phone.

2. Whenever possible have a physician or nurse present. A check with the players at the beginning of the season is an easy way to determine whether any parents are doctors or nurses. If any of them are, call and ask them for help during the season. They often are quite willing to help.

Carry with you Insurance Policy # and Insurance Forms.

The Basic Approach In First Aid

Always Remain Calm
It's not always easy, since the first sight of an injury can be upsetting. Nevertheless, helping to keep the injured player calm can sometimes be the best first aid you can render. This can only be accomplished if you remain calm yourself.

Never Assume The Role Of A Physician
The old saying, "It is better to be safe than sorry," is one that intelligent volunteer coaches will heed. Whenever there is any doubt, refer to a physician.

Never Move A Player Who Has A Serious Injury
This includes not sitting him up.

Use Good Judgment By Stopping To Think

Never Continue Play Of The Game When A Serious Injury Occurs

Blisters

A blister can be painful and limit the activity of a player. Keeping a blister clean and covered is of utmost importance, particularly if the blister breaks.

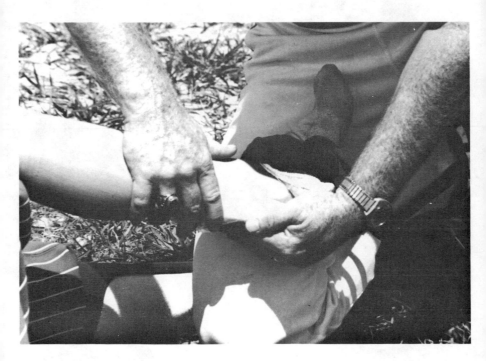

Nosebleed

Have the player sit and apply cold to nose (ice cubes or cold cloth) while pinching pressure at the bridge of the bleeding side of the nostril.

Foreign Body In Eye

Wash out eye with eye cleansing solution. If substance is not removed from the eye, refer to a physician. Cover the eye with a clean gauze pad and tape.

Jammed Finger

Apply a cold pack. Cold will help reduce the swelling. Refer to a physician for fracture.

Lacerations (Small Cuts)

First apply pressure to reduce bleeding. Then wash with a cleansing solution and apply sterile dressing and more pressure. If the cut appears to need stitches, refer to a physician.

Scrapes and Burns

Wash with cleansing solution that can be found in most coach's first-aid kits. Cover with clean gauze.

Unconscious Player

Do not move the player. Have one of your assistants call for an ambulance. Stay with the injured player and check to make sure that the breathing passages are clear.

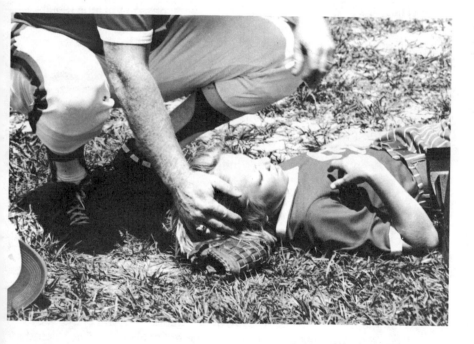

Muscle Pull, Sprains and Bruises

Apply ice or cold pack to the area to reduce swelling. If pain persists and the player is unable to move the injured part, refer to a physician.

As a general rule, in the case of sprains, strains or bruises to a joint (ankle, knee, etc.) remember the word ICE. It will be a good guide to recall how to treat bruises and sprains. I — Ice, C — Compression, E — Elevation.

Wind Knocked Out

Try to relax the player and encourage him to breathe easy.

Back Injury

If the pain is severe and numbness or weakness in the legs results, immediately send for an ambulance. Do not attempt to move the injured player. If the pain is slight, apply cold to the area.

Neck Injury

As with any back injury, do not attempt to move or sit the player up if the pain is severe, and especially if there is numbness or lack of feeling. Keep the injured player calm. Many times a head injury can be a neck injury; therefore, treat it accordingly.

Heat

Heat prostration is the inability of the human body to cool itself rapidly enough to keep up with the heat produced through exercise. In hot to humid weather the body cannot sweat and dissipate heat effectively. If an available source of water to replenish sweat is lacking, the problem is compounded.

Treatment should be directed at the immediate cooling of the body. Keep the player flat and move to a shaded, cool and well-ventilated area. If the player is responsive, small amounts of water may be given until an ambulance arrives.

Head Injury

Check with a flashlight to see if there is a difference in the size of the pupils, make sure that the injured player is able to breathe easily and have him carefully removed to the hospital on a stretcher. If one is not available, a door or a broad plank will serve the purpose. If a player is knocked unconscious but recovers quickly, he should not be allowed to return to the game or to further games until he has been thoroughly checked by a neurologist.

Loss of Airway

If a player is not breathing — from whatever cause — quick action is imperative. Make sure there is no obstruction in the mouth. With the player on his back, hold the head in both hands, one hand pressing the head backward and the other pushing the lower jaw upward and forward. Open your mouth wide, take a deep breath and seal your lips around the player's mouth while obstructing the nostrils with your cheek, or it may be necessary to have someone pinch the nostrils shut with his fingers. Blow steadily into the lungs for a few seconds and watch for the chest to rise, them remove your mouth. Inflation should be at the rate of ten per minute. The first six inflations should be given as quickly as possible.

Should the player be in a state of spasm or convulsion so that his mouth cannot be opened, it will be necessary to inflate the lungs by the mouth-to-nose method. Work from the side of the player. Make sure his head is extended. Open your mouth wide, take a deep breath and seal your lips widely on the players nostrils. Close the mouth by placing your thumb on the lower lip. If the head is not sufficiently extended, the solf palate will allow inflation through the nose but may prevent expiration. If this happens, part the player's lips with your thumb after each inflation.

After about 10 to 12 breaths, properly given, look for improvement in face and lip color, which should become more pink and less bluish. If there is no such improvement, quickly feel for the pulse at the side of the neck and at the wrist and listen carefully with the ear pressed to the bare chest over the heart. Look at the eyes and note the size of the pupils. If no heartbeat can be felt or heard and the pupils are dilated (large) or beginning to dilate, then external cardiac massage should be started immediately.

While receiving mouth-to-mouth resuscitation, the player should be lying on his back. Locate the lower half of the sternum or breastbone and place the ball of the hand on it, with the second hand covering the first. After each inflation of the lungs, apply six to eight sharp presses at the rate of one per second. The idea is to depress the sternum about one inch, with no more force than necessary. Remember in younger players less force will be needed than for adults.

When the heart starts beating, external cardiac massage should stop, but respiratory resuscitation should be continued until normal breathing is established.

Serious Bleeding

Even severe bleeding, such as occurs when a large artery in a limb is damaged, can almost always be stopped by direct pressure with the thumbs and fingers over that part of the wound from which the blood is coming. This should be done immediately. Sterile pads should be applied if possible, but don't wait while someone looks around for them. Better an infected wound than a dead player.

If the bleeding does not stop with direct pressure, a tourniquet should be applied without further delay. This may be a narrow folded triangular bandage or sling, a large folded handkerchief, a strip of strong cloth, an elastic belt or suspenders or a piece of rope or rubber tubing. It is applied above the wound around the upper arm or thigh, tight enough to compress the main artery and control the bleeding. The player should be taken to a hospital as quickly as possible.

Important Notice
On First Aid
To be sure of proper first aid application contact your local First-Aid Red Cross offices for the most up to date first-aid publications.

Techniques

throwing and catching the ball

Throwing a Baseball

Mechanics of throwing a baseball can be described in terms of **the grip** and **the arm and body motion.**

The Grip

For an accurate throw each time, the grip must be consistent. Spread half the length of the forefinger and middle finger over the top of the ball in the smallest area between threads. The two fingers remain close together with the thumb providing support underneath and centering the ball within the fingers. Holding the ball in this way creates a space between the palm and the ball.

1. **GRIP BALL CONSISTENTLY WITH FOREFINGER AND MIDDLE FINGER OVER TOP AND THUMB DIRECTLY UNDERNEATH.**

2. **KEEP FIRST TWO FINGERS TOGETHER AND HOLD BALL EITHER WITH OR ACROSS SEAMS. REMAINING FINGERS ARE BENT OR CURLED SLIGHTLY TO THE SIDE AND RELAXED.**

Arm and Body Motion

The ball must be thrown with a back rotation to travel in a straight path.

The Overhand Throw

Whenever possible use a full arm motion, a hip and shoulder half-turn, and a cocking and uncocking wrist action to release the ball. Release the ball slightly above and in front of the head as the hips and shoulders return to the starting position. This *overhand throw* is basic to outfield play and most often infield play as well.

Use a skip and step in the direction of the target when time permits.

1. EXTEND ARM BEHIND BODY WITH WRIST COCKED AND ELBOW BENT.
2. SHIFT WEIGHT TO FRONT LEG WHILE SWINGING THROWING ARM FORWARD.
3. PIVOT ON FRONT FOOT AND UNCOCK WRIST WITH A SNAPPING MOTION TO RELEASE BALL SLIGHTLY ABOVE AND IN FRONT OF HEAD.
4. FOLLOW THROUGH WITH THROWING HAND POINTING TOWARD TARGET.
5. SWING BACK LEG AROUND INTO BALANCED, READY POSITION.

The Sidearm Throw

With less time, *the sidearm throw* may be more advantageous although the full, overhand throw should be used if at all possible. The grip remains the same, but body action is abbreviated to place more stress on the throwing arm. Also control is often more difficult because the ball rotation or spin is changed. The ball may have a tendency to slide or sink.

After fielding a ground ball in the infield, you may not have the time to straighten to a full, upright position to throw out a runner.

In executing a sidearm throw apply the basic elements of the overhand throw. However, rather than swinging the throwing arm overhead from a layback position, swing the arm out from the shoulder and around parallel to the ground.

1. **GRIP BALL AS FOR OVERHAND THROW.**

2. **SWING ARM OUT FROM SHOULDER AND AROUND PARALLEL TO GROUND.**

3. **FOLLOW THROUGH TO TARGET.**

Catching a Baseball

The position of the glove when catching a baseball depends on whether the throw is above the waist or below.

Generally, the fingers of the glove point up when catching a ball above the waist and point downward when making a catch below the waist. For a catch at belt level, the fingers point more outward from the body than either up or down.

Catch the ball with both arms relaxed and extended toward the ball. As the ball is caught, the elbows bend to absorb the force of the throw. Catching the ball with a stiff arm results in a sore catching hand.

Cover the ball with the throwing hand as soon as the ball enters the glove to make sure the ball doesn't pop out and to throw quickly if necessary.

1. **GLOVE FINGERS UP WHEN CATCHING BALL ABOVE WAIST.**

2. **FINGERS DOWN WHEN CATCHING BELOW THE WAIST AND SOMEWHAT OUTWARD WHEN MAKING CATCH AT BELT LEVEL.**

3. **BEND ELBOWS TO ABSORB FORCE OF BALL.**

4. **COVER BALL WITH THROWING HAND TO SECURE BALL AND TO MAKE QUICK THROW IF NECESSARY.**

infield fielding

As a fielder, always assume that the ball will be hit to you. Think through in advance what you will do with the ball once you get it.

Assume a ready position so that when the ball is delivered to the batter, you move from a position of balance. This means that your weight is forward and over the balls of your feet.

Fielding Ground Balls in the Infield

Whenever you must move more than a few steps to field a ball, sprint toward the ball, then slow up to gain body control just prior to fielding the ball. Too often fielders move slowly at first, then accelerate when attempting to field the ball. Errors are often the result of this type of play.

Always when possible, ground balls should be fielded in the middle of the body. Carry the glove close to the ground with fingers pointing downward. Bend at the waist to get your head in position to follow the ball with your eyes.

With the glove just off the ground surface, the arms are relaxed and extended in front of the body. Your head must stay down so that you can follow the ball into the glove with your eyes. Glove the ball with elbows in front of your knees. Secure the ball with your throwing hand and begin throwing motion.

Again, the type of throw depends upon how much time you have to make the play. Whenever possible, use a full arm and body motion preceded by a skip and step toward the target. To throw more quickly or toss to a teammate close by, the sidearm or underhand throw may be used, eliminating the skip and step.

1. **READY POSITION**
   Face Batter
   Feet Comfortably Spread
   Knees Bent
   Weight Forward on Balls of Feet
   Eyes Fixed on Action

2. **ASSUME BALL WILL BE HIT TO YOU.**

3. **ANTICIPATE WHAT TO DO WITH BALL.**

4. **MOVE QUICKLY AND DECISIVELY FROM A BALANCED, READY POSITION.**

5. **FIELD BALL IN MIDDLE OF BODY WHEN POSSIBLE.**

6. BEND AT WAIST TO GET HEAD IN POSITION TO FOLLOW BALL WITH EYES.

7. CARRY GLOVE SLIGHTLY ABOVE GROUND SURFACE. KEEP HEAD DOWN. EXTEND ARMS IN FRONT OF BODY.

8. GLOVE BALL WITH ELBOWS IN FRONT OF KNEES. FOLLOW BALL INTO GLOVE WITH EYES.

9. SECURE BALL WITH THROWING HAND. MAKE OVERHAND, SIDEARM OR UNDERHAND THROW AS TIME PERMITS AND SITUATION REQUIRES.

Fielding a Ground Ball to Your Right or Left

Quite obviously, not all ground balls are hit directly to you. Most often they are not.

All basic fielding techniques apply when scooping up a ground ball to your right or left. Move quickly in line with the ball to field the ball in the middle of your body if possible. You may have time only to stretch for the ball.

Be sure to keep your eyes on the ball all the way, set up, then make a strong, accurate throw to the appropriate base.

1. MOVE TO BALL AS QUICKLY AS POSSIBLE.

2. KEEP EYES ON BALL.

3. THROW ACCURATELY. DON'T THROW BALL AWAY.

Tips for Fielding Ground Balls

Always charge balls hit slowly or with medium speed. As the old saying goes, "Play the Ball, Don't Let the Ball Play You!" This simply means that you have two options. Charge the ball and while doing so, choose the bounce or hop to field the ball. Or, lay back and wait for the ball, taking the chance that you may have to glove the ball on a difficult, in-between hop or that the ball might take an erratic bounce over your head.

Always move from a balanced, controlled position. Bend knees and back to keep body close to ground. Glove is out in front of your body with fingertips just off the infield surface.

Keep the ball in front of you. It is impossible to field ground balls cleanly every time. However, the hustling ball player very often avoids an error by scrambling after the ball to throw the runner out.

By knocking the ball down and keeping it in front, you stand a good chance of making the put-out with a quick recovery and throw. Once the ball gets past you, the chances of your recovering in time to throw the runner out are considerably less.

Keep your eyes on the ball. Often, in anticipation of making the throw, an infielder will take his eye off the ball at the last instant. Invariably in such a case, the ball skips under or over the glove. Keep your head down and "look" the ball into your glove.

Take time to set up before throwing. After ranging far to your left or right to field a ball, you may feel that you have to get rid of the ball quickly and rightly so. It takes just another instant to plant, then brace the rear leg for the throw to the base. By doing so, the chances are much less of your throwing the ball three rows up in the grandstand.

Taking a Throw at First Base

Because the **first baseman** receives many throws from infielders and often acts as a cutoff man on throws toward home from the outfield, the ability to range well and catch all types of throws is essential for playing this position.

Whenever a ground ball is hit to another infielder, the first baseman should sprint to first base and straddle the base to face the thrower.

Wait until the throw is made then stretch toward the ball while touching the base with the opposite foot. For a throw to the right-field side of first base, provided you are right-handed, tag the base with your right foot and stretch forward with your left leg to make a backhanded catch. This maneuver affords maximum range; however, some right-handed first basemen may prefer to step off with the right foot to face the ball more directly.

If you throw from the left side, merely step off with your right leg and tag the base with your left foot.

For a throw to the home-plate side of first base, as a right-handed thrower, step toward the throw with the left leg while tagging the base with the right foot.

Should you throw with your left hand, step with your right leg and tag the base with your left foot to make a backhanded catch.

1. **SPRINT TO FIRST BASE. TOUCH HEELS TO SIDE OF BASE.**
2. **WAIT UNTIL THROW IS MADE BEFORE STRETCH- ING TOWARD BALL.**
3. **LEAVE BASE ONLY IF THROW IS VERY WIDE, THEN TAG RUNNER OR BASE AFTER CATCH.**

4. **KEEP EYES ON BALL AND SECURE BALL IN GLOVE WITH THROWING HAND.**
5. **BE READY TO THROW BALL IF NECESSARY.**

Catching Low Throws into the Dirt

Throws into the dirt can be troublesome, even for the veteran player.

A quick pair of hands and good concentration are important factors in developing the ability to dig out low throws. Most important, keep your eye on the ball and do not jerk your head away when the ball skids into the dirt.

Throws to Second Base from First Base

After fielding a ground ball, tagging first base or taking a throw, a left-handed first baseman has the advantage of being able to throw to second without first taking a skip step.

A right-handed first baseman should take a short hop on the right foot toward second to get in position for throw to the infielder covering the base.

Whether throwing from the left or right side, the ball should not cross the path of the runner.

After fielding a ground ball and making the subsequent throw, sprint back toward first base then slow your momentum upon nearing the base to take the return throw for a double play if the situation merits.

37

Second Base/Shortstop Double Play

A **shortstop** should have the ability to move quickly to the ball, then make a strong, accurate throw after fielding the ball smoothly.

Both the shortstop and second baseman must learn how to tag second base and then throw quickly to first base.

Ideally, the ball should arrive about chest height slightly before reaching the base. The shortstop tags the base with the right foot, whereas the second baseman makes the tag with the left foot. Both players should take another step or so to move clear of the incoming runner while beginning the arm motion for throw to first base.

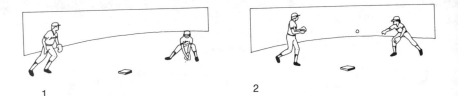

1   2

Shortstop/Second Base Double Play

A **second baseman** should be able to throw quickly and accurately without always stepping toward first.

This means that as a second baseman you must throw side-arm, across the body when the situation calls for a quick release. Such may be the case after fielding a slowly-hit ground ball or in making the pivot at second base for a double-play attempt.

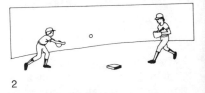

1   2

1. WHEN BEGINNING DOUBLE PLAY, CONCENTRATE ON FIELDING BALL CLEANLY. DON'T RUSH IT. OTHERWISE BALL MAY GO THROUGH YOUR LEGS.

2. THROW BALL TO REACH SHORTSTOP JUST BEFORE HE TOUCHES SECOND BASE. UNDERHAND THROW IS OFTEN BEST.

3. AS THE PIVOT MAN, THE SHORTSTOP TAGS BASE WITH RIGHT FOOT, MOVES CLEAR OF RUNNER AND THROWS TO FIRST BASE.

3

4

1. SAME PROCEDURE FOLLOWS AS WHEN SECOND BASEMAN STARTS DOUBLE PLAY.

2. SECOND BASEMAN CATCHES BALL AT CHEST LEVEL, TAGS BASE WITH LEFT FOOT AND THROWS TO FIRST BASE.

3. DISTANCE FROM BASE DETERMINES THE TYPE OF THROW AND SPEED OF DELIVERY.

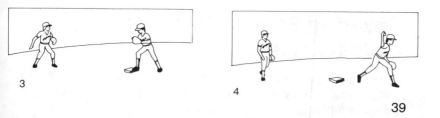

3

4

Third to Second to First Double Play

One of the most exciting plays in baseball is the third to second to first double play. Timing and accuracy are of the essence since the **third baseman** generally has to throw when the pivot man is still running toward second. Also, the ball must be delivered to a spot where the pivot man can handle it quickly, then throw to first.

The mechanics are the same as for the "Shortstop-Second Baseman Double Play." However, the greater distance element adds another variable affecting the time available to complete the play and the accuracy for successful execution.

Force-Out at Second Base

With two outs in the inning and a runner on first base, it may be more advantageous for a fielder to throw to second base for the third out than to throw to first.

On balls hit to the left side of the infield, the second baseman covers the bag; on balls hit to the right side, the shortstop covers.

To make the force-out, sprint to the bag and then touch your heels to the base as a first baseman does at first. From this point the mechanics of catching the ball and tagging the base are the same as those for making an out at first.

Force-Out at Third Base

Runners on second and first with one or nobody out would present one situation where a third baseman may be required to force the lead runner at third. Merely touch your heels to the bag and react as a first baseman would at first to make the out.

Covering Second Base on a Steal Attempt

The shortstop and second baseman should agree in advance, either vocally or by signal, who is to cover second base on a steal attempt.

Sprint to the base as soon as the steal is verified. Be in position to shift right or left in case the catcher's throw is off target.

As soon as catch is made, sweep your glove down and into position for the tag.

The Run-Down Play

In all run downs, it's important to keep throws to a minimum. With the ball in hand, sprint toward the runner.

If you cannot catch the runner, throw the ball ahead to a teammate. Stop and let your teammate chase the runner back toward you.

When the runner is four or five strides away, call for the ball, catch it and tag the runner out.

Catching a Pop Fly in the Infield

A pop-up or pop fly is a fly ball hit within the infield or one which an infielder attempts to catch.

Follow the same procedures as for catching a fly ball in the outfield presented in the following section.

Rather than throwing the ball immediately after making the catch, run the ball into the infield, unless, of course, a runner tags up and attempts to advance. However, such a move on his part may be a bluff to draw an erratic throw. Run first then throw if necessary.

outfield fielding

Catching a Fly Ball in the Outfield

One basic admonition underlies catching all fly balls in the outfield—**get to the ball quickly, get under it and wait.**

Turn quickly in the direction in which the ball is hit. It may take an instant to determine or "judge" the direction, speed and distance of the batted ball. Practice to make such assessments quickly and accurately.

Always check the direction and velocity of the wind. Such information is helpful in determining in which direction to turn for fly balls hit directly overhead or line drives. For an overhead fly ball, simply turn in the direction in which the wind is blowing.

On calm days, line drives curve toward the foul lines. A right-handed batter tends to hook the ball down the left-field foul line and slice it toward the right-field foul line. Conversely, the left-handed batter hooks the ball toward the right-field line and slices it to the left-field line. A particularly strong wind in one direction or the other may cause the ball to curve more or prevent it from curving as much.

Throw to Infield

In all cases, step and throw with a full, overhand arm motion, placing backspin on the ball so that the trajectory will hold true.

Pull the opposite hip and shoulder down to bring the throwing arm more overhand, thereby adding greater body action to the throw.

Practice long throws to second, third and home plate. Make throws so as to bounce once before reaching the base. Also practice throwing on the fly to the glove side of a relay man. Throw to hit a cutoff man on the fly as well.

1. GET TO BALL QUICKLY, GET UNDER IT AND WAIT.
2. CATCH BALL AT HEAD OR CHEST LEVEL WITH FINGERS POINTING SKYWARD.

3. PRACTICE JUDGING THE DIRECTION, SPEED AND DISTANCE OF BATTED BALLS. "SHAG" BALLS OFTEN TO KEEP SHARP.

4. IN ALL CASES WHEN MAKING THROW TO INFIELD, USE A FULL, OVERHAND ARM MOTION.

5. PULL OPPOSITE HIP AND SHOULDER DOWN TO GET MORE BODY ACTION INTO THROW.

6. PRACTICE THROWS TO BASES, ONE BOUNCE TO BASES. THROW ON THE FLY TO RELAY AND CUTOFF MEN. MAKE "LEVEL" TRAJECTORY THROWS TO INFIELD.

Catching a Ball Hit Overhead

Run with your back to the infield and turn your head to watch the ball over your shoulder. Don't back pedal. Get to the ball the quickest way. If time permits, turn to face the infield and make a normal catch at head or chest level with the fingers of the glove pointing skyward.

1. **TURN TO RUN BACK. DON'T SKIP BACKWARD.**

2. **IF TIME PERMITS, TURN BACK TO FACE BALL AND MAKE NORMAL CATCH.**

Fielding Sharply-Hit Ground Ball in Outfield with No Runners on Base

The tactics of fielding a ground ball in the outfield vary with the game situation although the basic techniques are the same as when fielding a ground ball in the infield.

With no runners on base, sprint to the ball then slow speed

Fielding Ground Ball in Outfield with Runners in Scoring Position

With a runner on base but not in scoring position, field the ball as a shortstop would in the infield.

With a runner(s) in scoring position, sprint to the ball without slowing up. Field the ball to the glove side of the body rather

when within three strides of the ball. Drop one knee to the ground to block the ball should it elude your glove.

1. **SPRINT TO BALL. SLOW SPEED WITHIN THREE STRIDES OF BALL.**

2. **DROP ONE KNEE TO BACKSTOP BALL SHOULD BALL ELUDE GLOVE.**

3. **SPRING UP AND THROW TO PROPER BASE OR CUTOFF MAN.**

than in front to avoid kicking the ball. Obviously, with the runner in scoring position this is an all-or-nothing type play.

1. **WITH A RUNNER ON BASE BUT NOT IN SCORING POSITION, FIELD BALL AS SHORTSTOP WOULD.**

2. **WITH RUNNERS IN SCORING POSITION, PLAY BALL TO GLOVE SIDE TO MAKE PICK UP AND THROW ON THE RUN.**

Tips for Outfielders

Concentrate on the game and anticipate what your next play would be should the ball come to you. In some games, outfielders may get few chances to field the ball. This may be particularly true if the pitcher is a low-ball pitcher with a good sinking fast ball. In such games it may be easy to "daydream" and lose contact with the game. Bear down on every pitch. Don't be caught napping.

Check the wind velocity and direction. As you take to the field each inning, take note of any wind changes. It's a little thing, but it could help you to catch a wind-blown ball which otherwise may cost your team a victory.

To catch a sinking line drive, keep your glove to the side of the body. As you dip down to catch the ball, chances are better that you won't kick your glove to jar the ball loose if your glove is out to the side rather than in front.

As an outfielder, call an infielder off a ball which you can catch. Your momentum carries you toward the infield whereas his momentum carries him away.

Also, to avoid colliding with fellow outfielders or infielders, get into the habit of "calling" for the ball provided that you intend to make the catch.

Don't hold the ball in the outfield. Always return the ball to the proper base or cutoff man as soon as possible to prevent runners from taking an extra base.

pitching

Control is the key to pitching success. For this reason the pitcher must be consistent in his windup and delivery.

Windup and Delivery

Place the forward foot (throwing arm side) in contact with the front edge of the pitcher's plate and the opposite foot directly behind the rubber.

To begin the windup motion shift your weight forward over the front foot. Bend slightly forward at the waist and swing the throwing arm back naturally. Note that the knees are also bent slightly.

As the throwing arm swings backward, shift your weight back, then as you bring your pitching arm forward again shift your weight forward appropriately. (Continued on Page 48.)

1. WIND UP BY SHIFTING WEIGHT FORWARD, BACK, THEN FORWARD AND SWING PITCHING ARM NATURALLY.

2. COCK REAR LEG FORWARD AND UP WHILE TURNING HIPS AND SHOULDERS ABOUT THE PIVOT LEG.

3. PUSH OFF PIVOT LEG AND STRIDE FORWARD WITH LEAD LEG. THROWING ARM SWINGS THROUGH LAYBACK THEN COMES FORWARD.

4. LEAD FOOT LANDS FLAT UPON MOUND TO POINT DIRECTLY AT PLATE, THEREBY ALLOWING BODY TO OPEN PROPERLY.

5. AS LEAD FOOT HITS GROUND, CONTINUE TO PROJECT BODY WEIGHT FORWARD WHILE PIVOTING HIPS AND SHOULDERS TO FACE SQUARELY WITH PLATE. AT SAME TIME, WHIP THROWING ARM THROUGH LEADING WITH ELBOW.

6. AS ARM COMES FORWARD, UPPER ARM IS APPROXIMATELY PARALLEL WITH GROUND AND ANGLE BETWEEN UPPER ARM AND FOREARM IS ABOUT 90 DEGREES.

7. SNAP WRIST TO RELEASE BALL, CONTINUE FORWARD MOTION WITH CONTROLLED FOLLOW-THROUGH, AND COMPLETE FOLLOW-THROUGH IN READY POSITION FOR FIELDING BALL.

8. READY POSITION
   Feet Nearly in Line
   Weight on Balls of Feet
   Knees Flexed
   Bent at Waist
   Head Up
   Eyes Fixed on Action

Windup and Delivery (continued)

Turn your hips and shoulders while moving the rear leg up and the throwing arm to the layback position.

Push off the rubber with your pivot leg and stride forward with the lead leg. Throwing arm swings through layback position and then comes forward.

Lead foot lands flat upon the mound, pointing directly at home plate. Stride and landing of the lead foot are most important in setting up the body to open or uncoil properly. Otherwise, a poor opening may mean that the pitch is delivered across the body rather than thrown with the body behind it.

As the lead foot hits the ground, continue to project body weight forward while pivoting the hips and shoulders to face squarely with the plate. At the same time whip your throwing arm through, toward the point of release. The elbow leads the arm motion.

Snap your wrist to release the ball. At release, the body, shoulder, arm, hand and back foot are moving forward. Continue forward motion with a controlled follow-through.

Complete the follow-through in position, ready to field the ball.

1. **COORDINATE FORWARD THRUST OF BODY, WHIPLIKE MOTION OF ARM AND SNAPPING ACTION OF WRISTS TO ACHIEVE OPTIMUM BALL VELOCITY.**

2. **THROW PITCHES THE SAME WAY EACH TIME AND PRACTICE FOR CONTROL.**

3. **FULL OVERHAND OR THREE-QUARTER OVERHAND DELIVERY PREFERABLE TO SIDEARM.**

4. **ALWAYS BE READY TO FIELD YOUR POSITION.**

Pitching from the Stretch Position

The stretch position is used with runners on first, second and sometimes with the bases full. From this position, the pitcher can throw to a base or deliver a pitch to the plate.

To assume the stretch position, stand with the pivot foot (foot on throwing side) against the rubber and the opposite foot forward and in line with the plate. Rest weight on pivot leg.

In the stretch move, bring the ball and glove together overhead, then lower both glove and ball (pitching hand) to pause at about belt level. As the stretch is made, the forward foot is brought somewhat closer to the pivot leg. Before throwing to the plate, a pitcher must pause at least one full second.

From this point the mechanics of the kick and delivery correspond to full windup except that kick might be abbreviated and undertaken more quickly with the pushoff from the rubber.

Note: Some youth baseball league rules do not provide for the stretch motion since leading from a base is not allowed. Check your league rules as the authority on this point.

The pitcher may move his head in any direction. Once a pitcher makes a move to first base, he must throw. Should he not throw, a balk is called and the runner is awarded second base. The pitcher can bluff a throw to either second or third base without penalty provided his foot is off the pitching plate. He must pitch to the batter once his shoulders and body are committed in that direction.

The move to first is merely a quick pivot and often a "short arm" throw. The throw must be accurate; otherwise, the runner may advance to scoring position.

1. **STAND WITH PIVOT FOOT AGAINST RUBBER AND OPPOSITE FOOT IN LINE WITH PIVOT FOOT AND PLATE. FEET ARE SLIGHTLY MORE THAN SHOULDER'S-WIDTH APART. REST WEIGHT ON PIVOT LEG.**

2. BRING BALL AND GLOVE TOGETHER OVERHEAD, THEN LOWER GLOVE AND PITCHING HAND WITH BALL TO ABOUT BELT LEVEL. PAUSE FOR AT LEAST ONE SECOND BEFORE DELIVERY TO PLATE. FAILURE TO DO SO RESULTS IN A BALK, AND RUNNERS ADVANCE ONE BASE.

3. LOOK TO PLATE, KICK AND PUSH OFF FROM RUBBER.

4. APPLY GOOD DELIVERY AND FOLLOW-THROUGH TECHNIQUE.

5. PICKOFF MOVE TO FIRST IS A QUICK PIVOT AND THROW.

6. GOOD FOLLOW-THROUGH HELPS ACCURACY.

7. TIMING AND COORDINATION WITH MAN COVERING BASE ARE MOST IMPORTANT FACTORS IN PICKOFF MOVE TO ANY BASE. PRACTICE THE PICKOFF PLAYS OFTEN.

Types of Pitches

Youth league baseball players are encouraged to concentrate on developing a good fast ball and change-of-pace while deferring work on a curve ball until the pitching arm and body are more fully matured.

The ball may be delivered with an overhand, three-quarter arm or sidearm motion. The sidearm motion puts more strain on the arm because it is more difficult to get maximum use of the body behind the pitch. Therefore, pitchers are encouraged to develop a good overhand and three-quarter arm delivery to take advantage of the momentum generated by good body action.

The Fast Ball

The *fast ball* is the mainstay of most pitchers' repertoires. Some fast balls sink, rise on or tail off depending on how the ball is held and how the pitch is released. The fast ball may be gripped across the seams at the widest point or across the seams at the narrowest point. The thumb usually contacts the seam directly under the fingers.

As you bring your upper arm forward, your upper arm is approximately parallel to the ground and the angle at the elbow is about 90 degrees. The ball leaves your hand slightly forward of the head. At this instant, every ounce of energy (body, arm and wrist snap) is imparted to the ball. The wrist snap occurs at the last crucial moment before delivery. At release, the ball rolls off the fingertips with a clockwise spin.

To make the fast ball sink, place the first and second fingers together between the narrowest seams of the ball, with thumb on the seam directly under the fingers. Apply pressure to the second finger.

To make the ball rise, place the first two fingers together where seams are farthest apart, with thumb on the seam underneath. Bring the arm straight overhead following through to the catcher's mitt.

The Change-of-Pace

The *change-of-pace* is pitched with a delivery to look like a fast ball, yet the ball travels much more slowly.

The farther the ball is held back into the hand, the slower will be the release. Spread first three fingers wide on the ball. Bring hand straight down quickly on release, as if pulling down a shade, giving the appearance of delivering the ball with speed.

Some pitchers retain the normal fast ball grip and achieve the change-of-pace with finger action at release. Fingers are relaxed on release to take some of the speed off the ball.

In both methods, it may be helpful to drag the pivot foot after releasing from the pitching rubber, thereby taking some of the body's motion from the ball.

Such a pitch is useful in keeping hitters off stride and setting up batters for the fast ball.

HOLD BALL IN BACK OF HAND WITH LITTLE PRESSURE BY FINGERS: OR, USE NORMAL FAST-BALL GRIP. RELAX FINGERS AT POINT OF RELEASE TO IMPART CHANGE-OF-PACE ACTION. DELIVER BALL TO LOOK LIKE FAST BALL. DRAG PIVOT FOOT TO LESSEN BODY'S POWER TRANSFER TO BALL.

The Curve Ball

A *curve* ball is thrown in such a way as to break and drop when nearing the plate.

If your players insist on using the curve ball, it is best that they learn to do it correctly. The first two fingers are held together with the second finger over the seams. Exert more pressure with the second finger and thumb than with the index finger.

As he delivers the ball, have your right-handed pitcher twist his pitching hand forward and clockwise. This motion is similar to releasing a "yo-yo" or slicing a pie. If your pitcher is left-handed, he should twist his hand counter-clockwise. This motion is coupled with a pronounced snapping action of the wrist.

The ball rolls off the outside of the index finger thus developing the spin necessary to cause the ball to break.

CURVE BALL SHOULD BE THROWN FROM SEAMS AND FROM ON TOP OF STRIDE SO AS NOT TO "CHOKE OFF" BREAK.

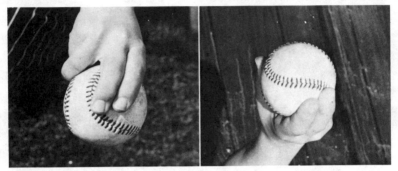

Tips for Pitchers

Run to condition your legs. Leg strength and endurance are vital to pitching. Often the legs will tire before the arm if the legs are out of shape.

Maximize the use of body motion and momentum to throw each pitch. Don't allow your arm to do all the work. Push off from the rubber and let good body action lend zip to your pitches.

Keep the ball hidden from the batter as long as possible before releasing. Hold the ball in your glove until the start of the body turn when the ball is withdrawn and thrown with full arm and body action. The glove should lead the throw, thereby further hiding the ball from the batter.

Gain confidence in your ability to throw the ball where you want it to go. Pick out a target—catcher's glove, knee, belt or whatever—and then keep your eyes on that target throughout the pitch. Move your head directly toward the plate so that the release of the ball occurs as far out in front of the pitcher's plate as possible.

Maintain a positive mental attitude while pitching. Don't let errors by teammates or the game situation "blow your mind." Concentrate only on throwing strikes and getting batters out.

Catching a Pitched Ball

Because the pitched ball has great velocity, a catcher has time only to shift one step left or right for pitches away from the plate. Therefore, a catcher must assume a position prior to the pitch which allows him to make this shift quickly.

The Ready Position

Begin in a squat position with feet comfortably spaced apart, knees turned out and left arm resting on thigh. The gloved hand extends beyond the left knee while the throwing hand gives the signals between the legs near the crotch.

After the signal is flashed for the pitch, rise up slightly from the squat position and spread your feet farther apart. The right foot is slightly behind the left foot.

The throwing hand should be relaxed with the fingers closed loosely around the thumb. Don't clench your fist.

1. ASSUME SQUAT POSITION WITH FEET COMFORTABLY SPACED APART, KNEES TURNED OUT AND LEFT ARM RESTING ON THIGH.
2. GLOVE HAND EXTENDS BEYOND LEFT KNEE WHILE THROWING HAND GIVES SIGNAL BETWEEN LEGS NEAR CROTCH.

Receiving the Pitch

The catcher's position should be as close as possible to the batter without interfering with him. From this position, the glove affords a better target to the pitcher. Also the catcher can handle low pitches and foul tips more easily.

Don't change the position of your hands until after the pitcher has started his delivery. If the pitch is below the waist, your gloved hand should be extended with the palm toward the pitcher and fingers pointing down. For a pitch above the waist, the fingers are pointed upward.

It is most important to receive the ball in the middle portion of the body. To catch the ball simply roll the right hand around the face of the glove to trap the ball in the pocket. Hands and arms "give" toward the body to cushion the impact. Fingers automatically encircle the ball.

The Throw

The game situation pretty much dictates how cautious a catcher has to be behind the plate and what type of throw he should make back to the pitcher or to one of the bases.

With runners on base, turn the hips and shoulders, drawing the ball and glove to the right side after the catch. This body turn will allow use of the entire body, should a throw to one of the bases be necessary. Use a step and full arm throw to a base. A quick but accurate throw is the primary desire.

3. **AFTER GIVING SIGNAL, RISE UP SLIGHTLY AND SPREAD FEET FARTHER APART. RIGHT FOOT IS SLIGHTLY BEHIND LEFT FOOT.**

4. **THROWING HAND IS RELAXED WITH FINGERS LOOSELY CLOSED AROUND THUMB.**

5. **ASSUME A POSITION CLOSE TO BATTER, BUT NOT SO CLOSE AS TO INTERFERE WITH SWING.**

6. **PROVIDE GOOD TARGET FOR PITCHER THROUGHOUT WINDUP AND DELIVERY.**

7. **CATCH BALLS BELOW WAIST WITH PALM OF GLOVE FACING TOWARD PITCHER AND FINGERS POINTING DOWN.**

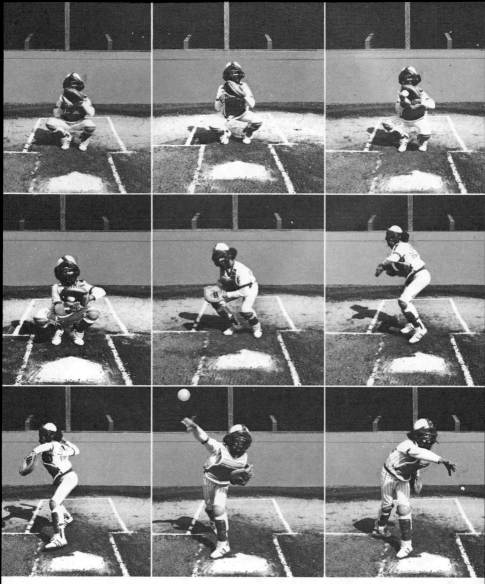

8. FOR BALLS ABOVE WAIST, POINT FINGERS UPWARD. AS FAR AS POSSIBLE, CATCH BALLS IN MIDDLE OF BODY.

9. SECURE BALL IN GLOVE WITH BARE HAND. HANDS AND ARMS GIVE TOWARD BODY TO CUSHION IMPACT.

10. AFTER CATCH, TURN HIPS AND SHOULDERS TO DRAW BALL AND GLOVE TO RIGHT SIDE.

11. FOR POWER AND ACCURACY, STEP AND USE FULL ARM THROW TO BASE.

How to Give Signals
and a Good Target

Catchers and pitchers should agree on signals which are easily understood. Finger signs usually serve best to signal which pitch is to be thrown. For instance, one finger pointing downward could be designated to mean a fast ball, two fingers down, a curve and three fingers, a change-of-pace. With a runner on second base, signals should be changed.

The catcher may use his thumb to indicate whether he wants the pitch delivered to the inside corner or outside corner, high or low. However, at the youth league level it's best that the pitcher concentrate on throwing strikes rather than attempting to hit a particular spot.

As a catcher, always give a good, steady target. Don't wave your glove around or relax your target just as the pitcher is about to deliver the ball. Doing so may distract the pitcher needlessly at the last second.

1. **WHEN GIVING SIGNALS, USE GLOVE TO BLOCK VISION OF OPPOSING COACHES.**

2. **KEEP KNEES FAIRLY CLOSE TOGETHER AND DON'T GIVE SIGNALS TOO LOW.**

3. **DON'T HURRY GIVING SIGNALS.**

4. **GIVE A STEADY TARGET. HOLD GLOVE SAME WAY FOR ALL PITCHES — FAST BALL AND CURVE.**

Catching Pitches Away from the Plate

From the basic catching position, merely shift by taking a step in the direction of the ball while holding the opposite foot stationary.

Of course for very wide pitches, more drastic action must be taken and most often very quickly. Sometimes, you may only have time to knock the ball down.

Blocking Pitches into the Dirt

With runners on base, the catcher must either catch the ball or at least keep the ball in front of him. Many catchers become particularly proficient in blocking low pitches to prevent runners from advancing.

Basically it's a matter of keeping your head down to watch the ball, getting your body in front of the ball (usually by dropping to your knees) and then hanging in there.

1. KEEP EYES ON BALL AND HEAD DOWN.
2. DROP TO KNEES TO GET BODY IN FRONT OF BALL.
3. BE READY TO SCRAMBLE FOR BALL SHOULD BALL GET AWAY.

Tips for Catchers

Learn opposing batters' strengths and weaknesses. To call pitches effectively, you should have some idea of what pitches cause a particular batter problems or in what position in relation to the plate a pitch would be most effective.

Keep signals simple. Signals should be seen only by pitcher, second baseman and shortstop.

Keep on top of the game. As a catcher, you are the key defensive strategist on the field. Your hustle and leadership inspire teammates to play harder.

Develop good rapport with your pitchers. Call time and go out to talk with your pitcher. Calm him down, buoy him up or merely check with him about a game situation.

Don't be a jumping jack. If you constantly bob up and down, you wear yourself out faster and bother the umpire.

On dropped third strikes, recover the ball, run toward the pitcher and throw to first base on the infield side. Dropped balls which roll away from a right-handed hitter should be retrieved and thrown to the foul side of first base.

hitting

Bat control should be the goal of every hitter. Such control is achieved through observing fundamental elements of good hitting.

Bat Selection

Choose a bat which is suited to your physical makeup and hitting style. It may be more advantageous to select a slightly lighter bat toward the end of the season, if the schedule has been particularly demanding and your body weight has been reduced significantly.

Bats vary according to length, weight and thickness of the handle. Choose a bat which feels comfortable in your hands. You may want to select a slightly heavier bat, normally the youth league player will use a 28 or 29 inch bat. Bat selection is an important factor in helping to achieve bat control.

The Grip

At the youth league level, the hands should be moved up from the end of the bat to achieve better balance and feel. Many batters use this "choking" action for better control when they get two strikes and want to protect the plate. Others use a choke grip for each swing.

Hold the bat with fingers, not in the back of the hands. The fingers should not grip tightly until the hands move forward prior to making contact with the ball.

1. **SUIT BAT TO BATTING STYLE AND PHYSICAL MAKEUP.**
2. **GRIP BAT WITH FINGERS, NOT IN BACK OF HANDS. TIGHTEN FINGERS AROUND BAT AS HANDS MOVE FORWARD TO CONTACT BALL.**
3. **"SHAKE HANDS" WITH BAT AS YOU PICK IT UP FOR PROPER KNUCKLE ALIGNMENT.**

The Stance

Again, you should select a stance which feels comfortable to you, whether it be a **parallel, closed** or **open stance.** You must be able to cover the plate when taking a forward stride to hit the ball. At the youth league level, start with parallel stance, then make adjustments from there.

After assuming your stance in the batter's box, make sure your knees are relaxed, not locked. Your hips should be relaxed also, square with the plate and parallel with your feet.

Arms should be comfortably away from the body with elbows bent and hands about shoulder height. The bat is back at an angle approximately halfway between the vertical and the horizontal.

Keep the shoulders as level as possible. Head should be steady with eyes fixed on the ball to follow it as long as possible from the time the pitcher starts his windup until the bat contacts the ball.

4. **CHOOSE A COMFORTABLE STANCE FOR YOU—PARALLEL IS BEST TO START WITH AT YOUTH LEAGUE LEVEL.**
5. **STANCE MUST ALLOW YOU TO REACH ALL AREAS OF THE PLATE.**
6. **READY POSITION**
   Hips Relaxed and Parallel with Feet
   Arms Comfortably Away from Body
   Hands About Shoulder Level
   Shoulders Level
   Head Steady
   Eyes Fixed on Ball

The Swing

It is important for each batter to know his own strike zone and when thrown a strike to attack the ball aggressively.

The forward arm guides the swing while the back arm lends power to it. The hitting swing is actually a coiling and uncoiling of the hips, shoulders and arms around a central axis, which is the backbone. It is a rhythmic timing of a progressive movement starting with a pivot of the hips and shoulders, flowing through the arms and wrists, generating power as it goes and culminating in a smooth follow-through.

The swing begins as the pitcher delivers the ball. Shift your weight back to the rear foot as the forward foot glides forward to meet the pitch. Simultaneously, the hips, shoulders, arms and bat pivot around the backbone axis. At the farthest extension of this pivot, your weight should be almost entirely on your rear foot.

Push off the inside of the back foot to begin the uncoiling movement and subsequently the swing. Brace the front leg instantly after it hits the ground.

With the planting of the forward foot, the hips pivot forward. The timing of the swing is such that the hands are well in front of the body before the bat is squared around to meet the ball. At this point, the weight is on the braced, forward leg. The entire left side of your body is firm as the ball approaches the strike zone.

Good wrist action is important from this point on. Such action is essential in bringing the bat around to meet the ball. Upon contact the wrists snap, then roll over for the follow-through.

With the wrist snap, the back hip shoots toward the ball as the forward hip swings away. The back foot pivots on the ball until the heel lifts off the ground. The toe stays on the ground to aid balance.

Continue the bat around naturally with a full follow-through. Let the weight of your body continue through and over the front foot.

1. AS PITCHER DELIVERS BALL, SHIFT WEIGHT TO REAR FOOT AS FORWARD LEG GLIDES FORWARD TO MEET PITCH. SIMULTANEOUSLY, HIPS, SHOULDERS, ARMS AND BAT PIVOT AROUND BACKBONE AXIS.
2. WITH WEIGHT ON BACK FOOT, PUSH OFF THAT FOOT TO BEGIN SWING.
3. BRACE FRONT LEG INSTANTLY AFTER IT HITS GROUND.
4. PIVOT HIPS FORWARD.

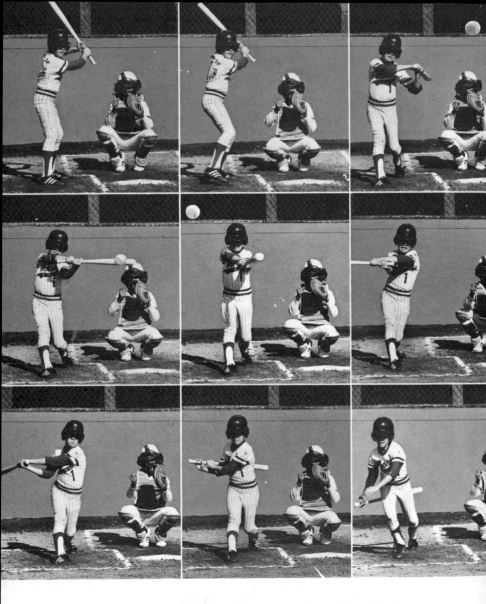

5. **HANDS WELL AHEAD OF BAT. WEIGHT ON BRACED, FORWARD LEG. LEFT SIDE FIRM AS BALL APPROACHES HITTING ZONE.**

6. **SNAP WRISTS UPON CONTACT WITH BALL. SIMULTANEOUSLY, SHOOT REAR HIP TOWARD BALL AND SWING FORWARD HIP AWAY.**

7. **ROLL WRISTS OVER AND COMPLETE SWING WITH A NATURAL, FULL FOLLOW-THROUGH.**

Tips on Hitting

Hold hands high and watch ball all the way in. Head and eyes should follow the ball as nearly as possible to the point of contact.

Hold bat straight up and down (perpendicular to the ground). Holding the bat in this manner allows you to swing down on a high pitch with the same motion as swinging an axe to cut down a tree. Swing upward on knee-high pitches as when playing golf. On belt-high pitches, swing straight through.

Push hands toward catcher as pitcher delivers ball. This move frees your arms from the body and facilitates timing.

Hold weight back as long as possible. Don't commit your weight forward too early or overstride the ball.

A compact, level swing or a slightly downward swing achieves best results. Low strikes require a slight upswing.

Learn to hit all types of pitches. Practice hitting pitches which give you trouble.

Concentrate on making contact with the ball. Hit the ball where it is pitched and learn to hit to all fields. Don't swing for the fences.

Bunting

A bunter's stance should be such as to allow coverage of the entire plate with the bat.

To bunt the ball in a sacrifice situation, assume the normal batting ready position as the pitcher begins the windup.

When the pitcher takes the ball out of his glove, pivot on the front foot to face the pitcher squarely by bringing the back foot up parallel with the front. Some bunters prefer to step back slightly with the front foot while turning and bringing the back foot up rather than pivoting with the front foot in place.

As you turn to face the pitcher, slide your top hand up the bat handle to a spot close to the trademark. Four fingers support the bat from underneath with the thumb on top.

The forearm of the forward arm is about parallel with the ground and forms nearly a 90-degree angle with the upper arm at the elbow. Body is crouched forward slightly, head is up, arms relaxed and bat is parallel with the ground.

Contacting the Ball

As the ball approaches, try to keep the bat as level as possible. Get the bat in front of the ball by raising or lowering your body from the knees and waist. Move your arms as little as possible.

Let the ball hit the bat. Upon contact the bat recoils into the "V" formed by the thumb and forefinger of the upper hand. This action deadens the impact and prevents the ball from bouncing too far.

1. ASSUME NORMAL BATTING STANCE. AS PITCHER TAKES BALL OUT OF GLOVE TO THROW, SQUARE AROUND TO FACE HIM.
2. AS YOU PIVOT TO FACE PITCHER, SLIDE TOP HAND UP BAT HANDLE TO SPOT NEAR TRADEMARK.
3. FOREARM OF FORWARD ARM ABOUT PARALLEL WITH GROUND, FORMING 90-DEGREE ANGLE WITH UPPER ARM AT ELBOW.
4. SACRIFICE BUNTING POSITION
   Body Crouched Forward Slightly
   Weight Forward
   Arms Relaxed and Bent at Elbows
   Bat Parallel with Ground
   Head Up
   Eyes on Ball

5. KEEP BAT AS LEVEL AS POSSIBLE AS BALL
   APPROACHES.
6. GET BAT IN FRONT OF BALL BY RAISING OR
   LOWERING BODY FROM KNEES AND WAIST.
   MOVE ARMS AS LITTLE AS POSSIBLE.

Bunting for a Base Hit

All bunting techniques apply, except that the batter should wait until the last moment before committing himself to the bunt.

When bunting for a hit, pick a pitch which will afford you the fastest start to first base. Then simply step toward the pitch with your forward foot and bring your bat into bunting position. Hold the bat firmly with your lower hand and rather loosely with the top hand to apply all bunting fundamentals.

Of course you realize that you have very little time to beat the ball to first base. At the instant you contact the ball your full attention should then be directed to getting to first base the fastest way. You really should not concern yourself with the ball at all beyond contact.

1. **CHOOSE A PITCH WHICH AFFORDS YOU A "JUMP" TO FIRST BASE.**

2. **WAIT UNTIL LAST POSSIBLE MOMENT BEFORE COMMITTING YOURSELF TO BUNT.**

3. **APPLY ALL GOOD BUNTING TECHNIQUES. KEEP BAT LEVEL AND EYES ON BALL.**

4. **AT CONTACT, DIRECT FULL ATTENTION TO RUNNING TO FIRST BASE. DON'T WATCH BALL.**

Bunting Tips

Unless "suicide squeeze play" is on, bunt only strikes. If the suicide squeeze is on, the ball must be bunted.

Action of the back hand should complement that of the forward hand. Hold firm with the bottom hand and more loosely with the top hand to provide the "softening" action necessary for a successful bunt.

All players should learn to bunt properly. Pitchers should practice bunting often since they frequently are called upon to execute the sacrifice bunt.

Because the left-handed hitter is a step or two closer to first base, the drag bunt may be particularly advantageous. Both right- and left-handed hitters with good speed can bunt for a base hit with good success, thereby getting on base to help the team and adding percentage points to their batting averages. Even slower runners can surprise the defense with a well-placed bunt.

baserunning

The all-out sprint between the batter's box and first base starts immediately after the ball is hit. No time should be lost in watching the ball. Even the time it takes to glance in the direction of the ball may mean the difference between reaching the base safely and being out.

Running to First Base

The swing of a right-handed hitter carries him away from first base; therefore it is best to start by pushing off with the left foot and thrusting the body in the direction of first base.

The first step is with the right foot and from there it is merely a matter of beating the throw to the bag.

The momentum from a left-handed hitter's swing carries him toward first base. Pushing off on the ball of the right foot and leaning the body in the direction of first base takes advantage of this momentum.

If it appears that it will be a close play at the bag, run just to the right of the foul line and tag the base in full stride. To insure that you do not slow up when nearing the base, select a spot some ten strides beyond the bag and run toward it.

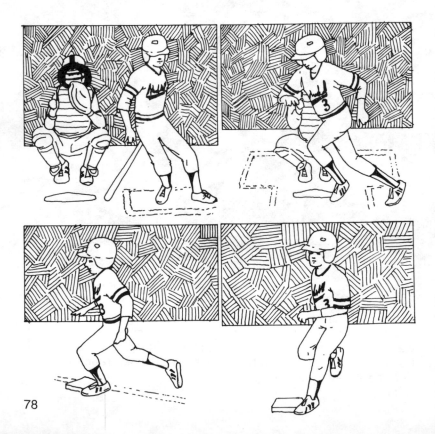

Your first-base coach will tell you if there is a chance for an extra base. If such is the case, run a tight circle pattern by moving out of the base line then arc back to tag the inside corner of the base in full stride. Keep on going if you think that you can reach second safely. If not, slow your run and return to first base quickly.

1. **RIGHT-HANDED HITTERS PUSH OFF WITH LEFT FOOT TOWARD FIRST, WHEREAS LEFT-HANDED HITTERS PUSH OFF WITH RIGHT FOOT.**

2. **RUNNING BASES IS MERELY A CONTINUATION OF FLAT ARC STARTED AT FIRST BASE.**

3. **WITH POSSIBILITY OF GOING TO SECOND, RUN TIGHT CIRCLE PATTERN AND TAG INSIDE CORNER OF BASE IN FULL STRIDE.**

4. IF GOING TO SECOND BASE IS NOT PRACTICAL, SLOW DOWN AND RETURN QUICKLY TO FIRST.

5. ON INFIELD BALLS RUN TO A SPOT SOME TEN STRIDES BEYOND BAG TO INSURE TAGGING BASE IN FULL STRIDE.

Taking the Leadoff

The type of lead which you choose to take depends on such factors as the game situation (Does it call for a steal or hit-and-run play?), the ability of the pitcher to make a move to first base, your speed and quickness and your general base-running ability.

The *one-way lead* is one in which you commit your weight in the direction in which you intend to run. Such a lead permits you to get a good start toward the next base. Obviously with your weight toward second, your return to first is somewhat more difficult, should the pitcher throw over there.

One suggestion is to take a slightly shorter lead so as not to draw the throw.

For a *two-way* lead, you assume a more balanced position allowing you to break for the next base or return to the former base with equal ease.

A *walking lead* is especially effective against a pitcher who is careless about checking a runner at first. Also, this leadoff should be used when leading off third base. Simply walk slowly toward the next base and then make your break when you determine the pitcher is going to the plate with the ball.

Regardless of the type of lead which you employ, once you have decided to run for the next base, run! Don't hesitate.

1. WHEN HOLDING A BASE, STAND WITH YOUR LEFT FOOT TOUCHING INSIDE EDGE OF BAG. KEEP FOOT ON BASE UNTIL PITCHER BEGINS WINDUP OR STRETCH MOTION.

2. TAKE LEADOFF IN DIRECT LINE WITH BASE. WATCH PITCHER CLOSELY.

3. BE PREPARED TO RETURN TO BASE. NOTE: WHEN LEADING OFF OF THIRD, WALK TO THE INSIDE (FOUL SIDE) OF FOUL LINE TO AVOID GETTING HIT WITH BATTED BALL. IF BALL ISN'T HIT, PIVOT INTO BASELINE FOR RETURN TO THIRD, MAKING CATCHER'S THROW MORE DIFFICULT.

4. TURN BODY IN DIRECTION OF RUN, PUSH OFF
   WITH BACK FOOT AND TAKE FIRST STEP
   WITH FORWARD FOOT.

5. ONCE COMMITTING YOURSELF TO RUN FOR
   NEXT BASE, RUN—DON'T HESITATE.

Sliding into a Base

A *slide into a base* is undertaken to avoid being tagged out.

Approach the bag with your body erect and your eyes on the base. Take off for the slide on whichever foot is most natural to you.

Immediately after taking off, bend the takeoff leg underneath to buffer the shock of landing on the ground, then raise the opposite leg well off the ground and extend it toward the base. Be sure the bent leg is turned sideways to avoid catching the spikes in the ground.

The brunt of the slide is absorbed on the lower part of the hip and back of the upper thigh. To avoid injury, do not slide on the foreleg portion of the leg. Contact the nearest corner or side of the bag with the extended foot. Once reaching the bag, let the momentum of the slide help you regain your feet to advance another base if possible. This type of slide, called *the straight-in slide, the pop-up slide* or *bent-leg slide,* is most basic.

In some cases on a close play at the base, you may prefer to remain in a prone position rather than continuing through to

the standing position. However, be careful not to stop so quickly as to twist your ankle or jam your leg.

1. APPROACH BAG WITH BODY ERECT AND EYES ON BASE. TAKE OFF ON WHICHEVER FOOT YOU PREFER.

2. AFTER TAKEOFF, BEND TAKEOFF LEG UNDERNEATH AND EXTEND OPPOSITE LEG TOWARD BASE. BENT LEG HELPS TO CUSHION FALL TO GROUND. SLIDE ON LOWER HIP AND BACK OF UPPER THIGH.

3. CONTACT NEAREST SIDE OF BASE.

4. LET MOMENTUM CARRY YOU FORWARD TO REGAIN YOUR FEET.

(The hook slide is not recommended because of possible injuries.)

Discipline
of Coaching

**Selecting Your
Team by Position**

**Coaching on Hitting
and Playing Positions**

**Basic Strategy
and Tactics**

Rules Simplified

Glossary

selecting your team by position

Remember, 11- to 15-year-olds do not really know which positions they can play best. Most of the time everyone wants to be a pitcher because Daddy or Grandpa wants him to.

There are physical requirements for each position. Here are some tips that may help you assign players.

Catcher

Look for a strong player. The catcher must have an excellent arm and be able to take "knocks." He should be a leader, a strategist of defense and have good physical ability.

Pitcher

Pitchers should have long arms and be able to throw hard. Short-arm prospects should be encouraged to try another position. With few exceptions short-arm players do not make good pitchers.

First Baseman

A left hander has an advantage here because most throws go to his right. The first baseman should have "size" to offer a good target for infielders and a "good glove" because he is in more plays than any other player except the pitcher and catcher. Make sure he is able to stretch and handle his body well.

Second Baseman

This player should have good range, a fast jump, sure hands and the ability to handle his feet to pivot. Of course, he should be a right-handed player. He must have excellent tools like the shortstop. Often he must share the same base. He must be able to pivot and needs a good arm to make a double play.

Third Baseman

If a player lacks speed and isn't a very big man third base may be his spot. A third baseman should have a good but not necessarily a great arm. His hands should be his best tool. A third-base prospect with good hands can do without speed and an extra-strong arm and still make the grade.

Shortstop

The most difficult position to play is shortstop. He has the most plays to make. This position requires your best infielder.

The shortstop prospect should have a good arm and excellent range with sure hands. He should be able to run.

Outfielders

Look for left handers because positions for them are limited. However, this doesn't mean right handers do not make good outfielders. Outfielders should have strong arms, speed and be able to swing a bat.

Your best arm should play right field since it involves the longest throw to the scoring base. If possible avoid playing a left hander in left field, since he has to turn to throw the ball when fielding balls going to the line or to throw to home plate. The weakest arm should play left field.

Ideally, your center fielder should be the best player in the outfield. He must have speed, range and a good arm and hands. He must be a take-charge player.

Coaching Players on Hitting and Playing Their Positions

Hitting

At times the long-ball hitter proves to be the "star" of a game, but the player who consistently punches out singles and doubles provides the real basis for team success. So often, hitters lacking great physical strength "swing from the heels" in attempting to become sluggers. A well-placed surprise bunt, a high bouncing infield hit or a smash through the infield pays off in game-winning runs.

A batter should maintain balance and be ready to meet the ball squarely. Often, a shorter stride provides for better body control. Good eye contact is a must along with hitting the ball in front of the body with a level swing. To encourage consistently good hitting, instruct your players to avoid dropping their shoulders as the pitch approaches. Shoulders should remain level.

Check the grip of your player. The bat should be held with the fingers, not deep within the palms of the hands. A good grip begins with picking up the bat. For best description instruct your players to "shake hands with the bat."

Most important, make sure that the weight and size of the bat are well suited to the physical makeup of the young player. Too often at the youth league level a heavy bat will cause the player to push the bat rather than swing it. To develop a smooth, strong swing, the youth league player should use a slightly lighter-than-normal bat while muscles are beginning to develop.

Teaching hitting is not an easy task! Some managers and coaches like to use broom sticks, shovel handles or garden hoses to swing at soda pop caps. This helps the batter develop good wrist action. Breaking the wrist with a "snap" to contact the ball is fundamental to good hitting.

Instruct players to keep shoulders level. Check to see that they don't drop their back shoulder when attempting to keep their weight on the back foot. Encourage your players to "keep their heads in there" and watch the ball all the way. Yes, it's possible to see the bat connect with the ball.

Pitching

Ability and control are a pitcher's prime assets. Neither is much good without the other, and both are useless without practice.

A youth league pitcher should develop a good change-of-pace to complement a strong fast ball. For the most part, pitches should be kept low. Some pitchers develop a rising fast ball or an off-speed pitch effective at shoulder height. The ability to vary the speed of each pitch is another important asset, one which can be acquired through dedication and practice.

One controversial question invariably comes up with any discussion of pitching at the youth league level. Does a young man hurt his arm by throwing curves too early?

The consultant to this book has coached at the youth level and above for many years. He says, "No, a young pitcher doesn't hurt his arm by throwing the curve." His rationale is that youngsters are going to try it anyway. Therefore, it is better for them to get the proper instruction on the techniques of throwing a curve ball than to do it entirely on their own.

It is his opinion that young arms are hurt by not warming up properly and pitching too often or without proper rest and conditioning. Your responsibility as a manager or coach is to make sure your pitchers are thoroughly instructed on all fundamentals of pitching including proper conditioning and rest.

Occasionally remind your pitchers of their responsibility to break up a double steal (runners on first and third). Your pitcher should take his stretch and then as the runner breaks,

back off the rubber. He should freeze the runner off first by taking a few steps toward him and then check the run on third. Should the runner on third break for the plate, the pitcher throws to the catcher. If the runner merely bluffs a run to the plate, the pitcher should throw to second to cut down the runner from first. If the runner on third gets caught in a run down, the pitcher must remember to back up the play.

On pick-off moves to any base, timing is the most important element. In youth leagues which allow leadoffs, well-executed pick-off plays can mean the difference in a ball game. Pick-off attempts to second base are usually handled by the shortstop. Very often a play is signaled by the catcher to the pitcher and shortstop. After the pitcher and shortstop each counts silently a specified number of counts, the shortstop breaks for second as the pitcher wheels and throws. On throws to third, very often the signal for the third baseman to break toward third for the throw is at the time when the pitcher touches the ball to his glove at the top of the stretch.

Physical conditioning is important to a pitcher as in the case of any athlete. Most managers and coaches prescribe running drills to keep pitchers' legs in shape. Strength and endurance to pitch for seven innings or longer are required.

A pitcher has an important role as a defensive infielder. Many games have been won through the pitcher's fielding ability as well as his pitching talent. To be successful, a pitcher must back up plays and cover bases when necessary.

Instruct your pitchers on these important points:

• **Teach your pitcher to toe the pitching rubber on the same side from which the batter is hitting.** If the hitter is right handed, the pitcher should begin his windup from the right side of the rubber. For left-handed hitters, the pitcher begins from the left side. This is a psychological and physical advantage for the pitcher since he bears straight down on the batter.

• **Once a pitcher releases the ball, he's no longer a pitcher, he's a fielder.** Instruct your pitchers to break for first base on all grounders hit to the left side. He must cover first base when the first baseman fields the ball, and then be prepared to throw to another base if necessary.

• **Encourage your pitchers to run hard,** not merely drift over to first. They should run down the line and touch the bag with the right foot. Often, it is difficult to run and catch the ball at the same time, but as often as possible your pitchers should try to make a normal catch without "snatching" at the tossed ball.

• **Always impress your pitchers with the importance of "looking" a bunted ball into the glove.** So often bunts are booted because the pitcher or infielder takes his eye off the ball at the last instant. A pitcher should take all bunts which he can get to. He should be instructed on these points: (1) He should break for the third base line with runners on first and second and less than two out; (2) A right-handed pitcher should field the bunt and throw in one motion; (3) A left-handed thrower must field the bunt, pivot to his right and throw to the infield side of first base to avoid hitting the runner; (4) The

92

pitcher must know who is covering second in case he fields a bunt and has to throw to second base; (5) After fielding a bunt, a pitcher should throw to the infield side of third base.

- **Remember a pitcher must:** (1) Learn how to pace himself, (2) Stay ahead of the hitters, (3) Have hitter hit his pitches, (4) Know hitters' weaknesses, (5) Realize what pitches are working best on a particular day, (6) Always know the count and score, and (7) Never shorten up on the pitching motion and delivery.

The Catcher

As the workhorse of the ball club, the catcher instills confidence in the pitcher and guides him and other teammates on the field.

His job requires studying opposing batters so as to call pitches which capitalize on the batters' weaknesses. Because of his commanding position behind the plate, the good catcher encourages his teammates, keeps them hustling and makes sure they are in position to play the batter properly.

The experienced catcher blocks pitches, throws off his mask quickly to catch pop flies and guards the plate forcing the runner to run into the tag. A good receiver is relaxed and in command of his emotions at all times.

A catcher has certain responsibilities to other players within the infield:

- **Regarding the pitcher, a catcher should:** (1) Remind him to break toward first on balls hit to the left side. (2) Make sure he knows who is covering second base. (3) Call out the base for the pitcher's throw after fielding a bunt. (4) Remind the pitcher to back up third and home on fly balls and singles. (5) Remind him occasionally of the score and the importance of an out as you do with all infielders.

- **Concerning the first or third baseman, the catcher should:** (1) Remind the first baseman that a particular runner(s) has outstanding speed. (2) Call out to him the play on bunts and double plays. (3) Yell out when to cut off the ball thrown from the outfield. Inform him of how much room he has when nearing the dugout on a pop foul. (5) Always give a good target to infield side of the base line for the first baseman to make his throw.

Work with your receivers to help them become "complete" catchers.

- **On ground balls in the infield,** remind your catchers to back up first base. A good catcher can really show he's hustling on this play. When the third baseman fields a bunt with men on first and second, the catcher must cover third base.

- **A force-out at home is handled in much the same way as a force-out is at any base.** Coach your catchers to stand with home plate between their feet. Since home plate is not a raised base as the others are, some catchers feel more secure by placing one foot on the base. Whereas the range may not be as great as with the "straddle method," there isn't the chance of missing the base with the foot. After making the force-out at the plate, impress your catchers with the importance of getting rid of the ball quickly to first to complete the double play, should there be fewer than two out.

- **When taking throws from the outfield,** in most cases it's more expedient for the catcher to let the ball come to him than going out to get the ball, then scrambling back to make the tag.

• **To block out the plate effectively,** the catcher should stand in fair territory at a 45-degree angle to each foul line. Instruct him to crouch in a low position. Most catchers prefer to give a runner one corner of the plate to slide toward. Others prefer to block off the whole plate. The ball should be caught and moved into position for the tag with a smooth, flowing motion.

• **When fielding bunts** instruct your catchers to push the ball into the glove. They should never field the ball with the bare hand. On bunts down the third base line, coach your catcher to field the ball with his back to the first baseman. From this position he can throw much more quickly since he doesn't have to make an awkward pivot back to his right before throwing. Remind your catchers that they have to scramble after the ball since they don't as a rule have much time. Often a catcher must throw quickly using an underhand or sidearm motion from a crouch position.

● **On fouls,** coach your catchers to watch the ball leave the bat without blinking. They should locate the ball as soon as possible, then throw the mask in the opposite direction. Balls hit in the home plate area have a tendency to drift toward the infield due to the spin on the ball. Therefore, the best procedure is to have your catcher turn his back to the infield, give the ball plenty of room and let it drift into him. When possible, a catcher should let another infielder catch the ball since most often that fielder has a better perspective. In catching the ball, coach your catcher(s) to position himself as though the ball would hit him on top of his head. He should then extend his glove in a parallel position to the ground. From this level plane, the ball bounces upward should it not be caught, therefore giving the catcher a second chance to make a grab for it.

● **In breaking up double steals,** the catcher's first move is to look the runner back to third, then throw to second base. Then next time he may choose to fire the ball to third in hopes of getting the runner in a run down.

● **The catcher(s) on your team should be the quarterback.** He should know when to expect a bunt, when to call time out for a conference with the pitcher or infielders, when to pitch out and when his pitcher is losing his "stuff." He should be close to his manager, detect weaknesses in the opposition, keep control of his emotions and call the plays in front of him. He must direct outfielders should a move for a particular hitter be necessary. He should remind everyone of the number of outs in the inning by holding up his fist to indicate no outs and one or two fingers to show a corresponding number of outs. He's a holler guy who shouts encouragement to his teammates and psyches out opposing hitters.

The First Baseman

The first-base position is one of the busiest in the line-up and involves more than being able to catch and hold a thrown ball. Either in a direct or assisting role, the first baseman is involved with almost every play. He must know how to handle bunts, when and how to throw the ball and back up throws to home plate, how to take a relay from the outfield, when to hold the runner on first base and many other phases of the game.

A good first baseman moves around and shifts his position when necessary. Touching the bag when taking the throw is a mechanical action which should become second nature. While many short players have become good first basemen, the taller player has a reach advantage important to playing the position well. The left-handed player also has an advantage in that he can throw to other bases more easily.

One further point: the successful first baseman catches the ball with both hands when possible. He saves the spectacular one-hand grab until the time it really counts.

- **Have your first basemen practice fielding their position** while playing deep as for a left-handed power hitter, halfway in and in close. Where your first baseman plays a hitter is related to such factors as whether the batter is right or left handed, how much speed the hitter has and the situation in the game — bunt, hold runner at first, play at the plate, etc.

- **Like the third baseman, the first baseman should always keep the ball in front** of him even if it means playing the ball off his chest, pouncing on it and throwing the runner out. As long as the ball is in front of him, he still has a chance for the out.

- **When possible, the first baseman should make the play himself** after fielding a ground ball. Otherwise, the first baseman should take a step and toss easily, chest high to the pitcher covering the bag.

● **The first baseman goes to the bag and sets up with both heels against the base.** He picks up the flight of the ball and stretches to meet it.

● **For wide throws up the base line,** he stretches to his left and tags the base with his right toe.

● **On high throws,** instruct your first baseman to leap, make the catch and then come down on the back portion to leave the base line open for the runner to avoid the possibility of a collision.

● **For wide throws to the outfield side,** he stretches to the right and touches the base with his left toe.

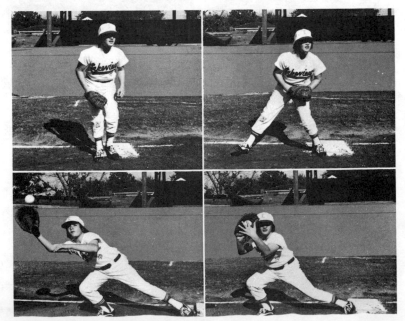

• **When holding runners on,** your first baseman should provide the pitcher with a good target to the fair-territory side of first between the base and the runner. After catching the throw, he can merely drop it on the runner sliding back. Have your first baseman position himself in fair territory, to the home-plate side of the bag. With the pitch, he moves toward second in direct line with the bases. When not holding the runner on, he should play back, but not toward second base. On dropped third strikes, instruct him to give the catcher a target to the inside of the base in foul territory.

• **When throwing to second on a double play,** your first baseman should throw to the shortstop on the right-field side of second.

• **Instruct your first baseman on his relay and cut-off responsibilities.** On any ball hit down the right-field line and into the corner, the first baseman goes out to line up the throw and make the relay. As a cut-off man he lines up approximately 40 to 50 feet from the catcher and in line between the thrower and the catcher for throws from right field to home, right center to home and center to home.

• **Again like the third baseman, the first baseman should protect the line** against an extra-base hit with the score tied or close in late innings.

The Second Baseman

With many baseball teams relying on left-handed hitters, the second baseman gets his share of action.

Often, second base is a pivot position for double plays. A second baseman shifts his feet quickly and throws accurately. Speed and timing are key factors to a successful double play.

Points to Remember When Coaching Second Basemen:

• **Like the first baseman, the second baseman should practice fielding and throwing** from various depths and proximities to second base. Drill your second baseman on moving from a ready position with weight on the balls of the feet, feet a shoulder's-width apart and arms relaxed. A second baseman should always move with weight under control, glove out in front of body and eyes on target. He should "look" the ball all the way into his glove. Like the first baseman he still has a chance for the out provided that he keeps the ball in front of him. From various positions, have him throw quick sidearm throws and basic overhand throws. Emphasize his planting the right foot for throws to first after ranging far to his right for the ball.

● **Work with your second sackers in making the tag out at second.** Two techniques are widely employed — shoving the ball deep within the glove and closing the fingers around it or holding the ball in the bare throwing hand within the pocket of the glove. The latter method requires more time to set up but usually provides a better defense should the runner attempt to kick the ball out of the glove. Regardless of which method is used, the runner should never see the ball as a target to dislodge.

● **The second baseman must have his body under control when acting as pivot man on the double play.** Drill him on making the play naturally, not mechanically. His footwork is important. With practice he should make the foot adjustments while looking at the throw the whole way — not at the bag. Coach him to play slightly closer to the base with a speedy runner on first. On balls hit reasonably close to second base, he should field the base, pivot to his right, and make his toss (underhanded or directly from the glove). For balls hit wide of second, he should field the ball, pivot to his left and throw smartly to second.

• **Should the shortstop bobble the ball in starting a double play,** coach your second basemen to position themselves as a first baseman does in relationship to the base to make the force-out.

• **When called on to cover first on bunts, emphasize getting over there** to catch the ball while stationary, not on the run. Footwork is the same as employed by the first baseman in making the catch. Make sure your second basemen know that they are to back up throws to first from the pitcher or catcher. A second baseman also backs up on pick-off throws — catcher to first, catcher to second and pitcher to second.

• **How far a second baseman ventures into the outfield** to make the relay depends on the strength of his arm. A second baseman is responsible for relays from left center field and for backing up the first baseman during his relay play on a sure three-base hit. In making the relay throw, the catch is made on the left side of the body while he is running back toward the infield. The momentum then carries the relay man into throwing position for a strong throw.

• **A second baseman should always remember:** (1) To charge slowly hit ground balls and snap throws to first base; (2) To keep eyes on the ball and stay down on grounders, to knock down tough chances, recover and throw out the runner; (3) To back up teammates and hustle out to make a relay to the proper base; (4) To coordinate with the shortstop on covering second base; (5) To practice catching "Texas League" pop flies and whirling to make the throw; (6) To drill with the first baseman in strengthening the right side defense.

The Third Baseman

The third baseman is keeper of the infield's "hot corner." He must handle everything from sizzling line drives or one-hop shots to slowly-rolling bunts. Above all he must keep his mind on the game so as to anticipate the next play.

A third baseman's most important physical asset is his ability to field a ball and throw to first base in one motion.

Runners on first and second base put great pressure on the third baseman to think and act quickly. Often, he must range far to the left to make the play in front of the shortstop, back up teammates and take throws for plays at third base.

Occasionally, review these points with your third basemen:

● **Have your third baseman position himself after making these assessments:** (1) Is the batter left or right handed? (2) How hard does your pitcher throw and does the batter have good speed? (3) Does the situation call for a sacrifice, a squeeze play or "drag" bunt? (4) Does the defensive strategy call for a double-play attempt, a force on the lead runner or a play at home plate?

- **With runners on base, playing bunts at third base** often calls for split-second decisions. When a runner is on first with less than two outs and especially with none out, instruct your third baseman to cheat toward home as the pitch is made to field the attempted sacrifice if necessary. The catcher must cover third. With runners on first and second and less than two out, the third baseman should hold his position on the lip of the infield grass to see if the pitcher fields the ball. Should the pitcher make the play, the third baseman covers third as a first baseman does at first. If the ball gets past the pitcher, the third baseman fields the ball and makes his throw to first base.

- **Like the shortstop going into the "hole" for a grounder, the third baseman** must plant his right foot before throwing to second or first.

- **When taking throws from the outfield at third,** stress the importance of shifting from a ready position to block the ball on bad hops. The ball must be blocked from getting through to allow the runner to score. The third baseman should set up on the outfield side of the base when taking throws from left or center field.

With the throw coming from right field, the third baseman should cover the bag from the infield side. (See below)

• **A third baseman becomes a cutoff man and the shortstop covers third** when a ball is hit to left field and a runner is on second or on a fly to left and a runner is on third. With a runner on third and the infield pulled in for a play to the plate, should the ball be hit within the infield, the third baseman breaks toward the third-base line. If the catcher traps the runner coming from third, he then can throw quickly to the third baseman for the tag.

• **On a pick-off play to third,** the third baseman should make his break to cover third as the pitcher touches the ball to his glove at the top of his stretch. When taking a throw from the catcher in an attempt to catch the runner off third, instruct your third sacker to give the catcher a target to the fair side of the bag.

• **A third baseman must be mentally alert ("heads-up") at all times.** In late innings, he must protect the line to prevent extra-base hits. He should alert the pitcher and other infielders that a bunt is in order. When an intentional pass is being offered a batter with a runner on third, he should strike up a conversation with the runner to hold him near third in case the ball gets by the catcher. In such an instance the runner has much farther to run than if he took his normal leadoff.

The Shortstop

Because he must cover so much area and participate in such a wide variety of plays, the shortstop position often is considered to be the most demanding within the infield.

Without hesitation, the shortstop must react to any situation — run back quickly for pop flies, charge slowly-hit grounders, make strong, accurate throws to first base from deep in the "hole" as well as many other plays.

The shortstop should always play the ball and not wait for the ball to play him. Hard smashes have to be handled as best they can, yet often a quick recovery and good throw retire the runner.

● **As the pitcher begins his windup, the shortstop should move into a relaxed, ready position** with hands and arms dangling downward, bent at waist, weight on balls of feet and heels off the ground. Have your shortstops and other infielders practice moving from this ready position to make all plays with a confident, fluid motion.

● **In a double-play situation when near the bag,** the shortstop should toss the ball underhand so the second baseman may catch the ball at chest level. When going away from second to field the ball, the shortstop has to field and throw the ball with something on it, in one motion.

- **As the pivot man on a double-play attempt,** the shortstop tags the base with his right foot. In a routine, double-play situation the shortstop drags his foot across the bag, moves clear of the runner on the right-field side and makes the play to first. When the shortstop is nearer the base as the play begins, he may need only to kick the base with his right foot or use the bag as a foothold to make the throw. Your shortstops and second basemen should practice often to get their timing and footwork coordinated. On a double-play throw from the first baseman, the shortstop should touch the base with his left foot on throws to the infield side and with his right foot on throws to the outfield side.

- **When taking the throw from the catcher on a steal attempt,** the shortstop should move in slightly toward the pitcher as he sets up to cover the base. At the youth league level, the shortstop should make the play from a position to the infield side of the base rather than from a straddle position over the base. Later on, the players can develop the straddle technique.

- **When a double steal is attempted,** the throw is taken just in front of the base so that the return throw to home can be made quickly.

- **On a pick-off play with the pitcher,** instruct your shortstop to move in back of the runner to a position where he can receive a throw or return to his fielding position should the pitcher go to the plate. Usually, the shortstop has a signal that he'll break for the bag and be there by the time the ball arrives.

- **With a throw coming from right field to third base,** the shortstop should position himself to cut the ball off and throw back to second if necessary.

- **The shortstop acts as relay man** on throws from left field and left center to third base. How far he goes out to receive the throw from the outfielder is determined by the strength of his throwing arm.

The Outfielders

The outfielder must always be alert as to what to do with the ball, should the ball come to him. He should be mindful of the game situation at all times.

A moment's delay may permit a runner to take another base, or worse yet, score the game-winning run. An outfielder also should note these factors:

- **To gain the opponents' respect,** drill your outfielders to develop a strong, accurate throwing arm. Have them keep the trajectory of the throw low to the ground. On throws to home plate, they should aim for the pitching mound and bounce the throw into the plate. Often remind your outfielders to throw ahead of the runner.

- **Coach outfielders to block ground balls** to prevent balls dribbling through their legs. Encourage them to back up teammates and never to assume that another outfielder will be able to get to the ball. Also, they should be encouraged to catch the ball with both hands, and save the spectacular one-hand grabs for when it really counts.

● **To avoid collisions in the outfield,** make sure your outfielders call for fly balls. When chasing fly balls near the fence, instruct your outfielders to feel for the fence with the throwing hand, then come in if necessary to make the catch. Having them develop this technique helps avoid injuries resulting from crashing into the fence. The outfielder can concentrate on catching the ball rather than worry about running into the wall.

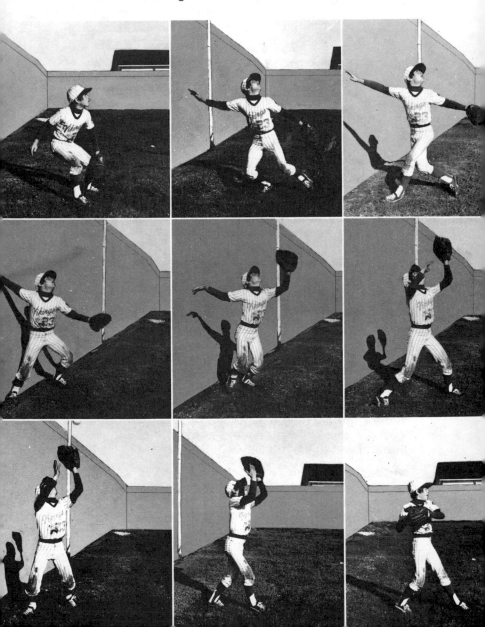

Basic Drills

Pair up and have the man with the ball wait until his partner gets his weight forward on his toes and places his glove on the ground with the fingers down. Then the man with the ball throws or rolls the ball directly at, left or right of the glove man. Following the catch, the partners reverse the procedure.

Quick Hand Drill

Hand-to-eye coordination is a necessary skill especially for infielders. The Quick Hand Drill is a quick exchange of the ball rolled on the ground between two players. Hustle is a key factor in this drill.

Four-Man Infield Drills

One player hits ground balls while a second player stands next to him and acts as a first baseman. A third player fields the ball and throws to the second player. A fourth player is the back-up man behind the third player. After ten balls are fielded, the men change positions.

Infield Warm Up Drills

Pitchers, catchers, first and third basemen work on fielding bunts and balls hit between the mound and first or third. The second baseman and shortstop work on the double play. The throw to first should be caught by someone standing twenty feet away from first base to avoid interfering with the other drill.

Learning to get off quickly is a must for a baseball player. The reaction drill starts with one player facing the other. The player with the ball simply lobs the ball over the other player's head at a reasonable distance. The pursuing player reacts as quickly as possible in trying to bring in the catch.

Four-Man Outfield Ground Ball Drills

In this case, the outfielder will practice (1) blocking the ball, (2) controlling his charge by sprinting to the ball and slowing as he fields it, and (3) making an all-out charge in which he practices fielding the ball on the glove side of his body while at an all-out sprint. Again the first player acts as hitter; the second acts as the relay man or baseman; the third is the fielder; and a fourth, back-up.

Situation Drills

Place bases 30 feet apart. Position all nine defensive men. Use walkers instead of runners. All throws must be lobs and fielders must walk after the hit (accomplished by a coach at the plate). Since all the players are close together, it is easy to explain to everyone what his duties are on each play.

Pepper Drill

This is a good drill for all players. The batter hits short, choppy balls to the other players. The drill helps the batter learn to coordinate placement hits to various directions and in turn helps defensive players develop quick reaction.

Two-Man Batting Drills

A barrier and a net or canvas are required for this drill. One player underhands the ball to another player who hits it into the net. It is wise to start the season practicing hitting to the opposite field, insuring that the hitter keeps his head and eyes on the ball.

Getting Your Players Ready for the Game

When it comes to preparation, a youth league baseball game is no different than any other sport at any level. You and your players must be organized. If not, you will have disorder, which can result in an unhappy experience in coaching.

You must:

1. Make sure the players know the site and time of the game.

2. Make sure all players have transportation to the field.

3. Check that all the equipment (catcher's mask, scorebook, first-aid kit, etc.) gets there.

These are only a few of the details a youth league coach has to keep on top of.

Most important, keep a list of emergency telephone numbers handy. If possible, a physician should attend games. If this is not practical, his phone number and that of an ambulance service should be accessible. Always have change to make a call and know where the nearest telephone is located. These telephone numbers and change can be stored easily in your well-stocked first-aid kit.

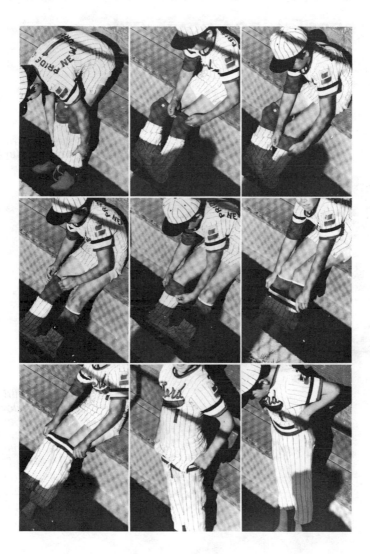

On the following page, proper dress requirements are listed. In baseball, special attention should be directed to getting your catchers outfitted properly: (1) Masks should fit and allow an adequate line of sight. (2) Body protectors should contour to the body and protect the shoulders. An adjustable harness keeps the protector in place. (3) Leg guards must be of proper size. They should fit over the knee and extend down to fit over the instep and ankle. Various sizes are available. (4) Helmets are mandatory in most leagues to protect against foul tips and the swinging bat. (5) All catchers must wear an athletic supporter and cup.

Proper Fitting Equipment

1. *Caps . . . of proper size will stay in place and shield players' eyes from the sun.*

2. *Clothing . . . should fit fairly close to the body but allow freedom of movement. Players should consider wearing shorts (not briefs) or sliding pads under their pants for additional leg protection in sliding.*

3. *Shoes . . . should be the proper width. The instep should fit snugly but not uncomfortably. When laced the shoe should not be able to be pulled away from the heel.*

III Fitting Equipment

1. *Caps . . . that are too large can slip over the eyes during a critical point at the plate or in the field. Keep hair under the cap and off the face.*

2. *Clothing . . . Shirts must be tucked into pants. If the pants do not have an elastic waistband, wear a belt. A big, loose-fitting uniform can affect your play.*

3. *Shoes . . . that are too big cause improper weight distribution over the cleated area. Ill-fitting shoes cause blisters.*

Putting on the Helmet

While it may seem to be a simple process, sometimes putting on a helmet can be a problem for the novice player, especially when the hair covers the eyes.

To avoid unwanted hair in the eyes, the front portion of the rim should be pressed against the forehead first, then the remaining portion of the helmet pressed back and onto the head.

Batting helmets are available in various sizes. Have a good assortment of these sizes to fit your players.

A helmet that doesn't fit properly most likely will be a distraction to your hitter, giving the opposition an advantage.

Considerations in Making a Batting Order

Organizing a good line-up is very important. Each player should meet the particular requirements of his position in the batting order.

The Leadoff Batter

This position requires a player who likes to take pitches and has a good "batting eye." He should be able to hit with two strikes so he can get an early look at the pitcher, acting as scout for the rest of the line-up. He reports if the pitcher is fast, has good or bad breaking pitches and so on. His job is to get on base. He can be allowed to run early to test the catcher's arm, which helps the manager decide later in the game whether to bunt or run.

Second Hitter

In this position bat control is important. The player should hit the ball late and to the opposite field. He should be a good bunter to allow the manager to bunt for an important run if it is needed late in the game. Early in the game he may be a hit-and-run man.

Third Batter

This slot should be reserved for your best hitter. He must be able to get a hit with two outs to allow the power hitter a chance to score him from first with an extra-base hit. He also must be able to knock in runs with men on base. This hitter must do it all with the bat. He should be an excellent hitter with power and know the strike zone. He seldom or never steals a base. His speed is important since he must score from first on an extra-base hit with two outs.

Fourth Batter

Your power should bat here. He should be a home-run hitter or someone with the ability to score a runner with an extra-base hit. Power is the overriding requirement of this position. This player does not have to be a good runner.

Fifth and Sixth Hitters

Again, these players should have power but also they must be good or fair hitters. These are the positions where the most designated hitters will probably bat if the new rule in baseball stands.

Seventh Hitter

This hitter is almost as important as the leadoff hitter except in third- or sixth-inning situations. If he reaches base he will probably steal so he must have excellent speed. You don't want to bunt him to second with your eighth-hole hitter because your pitcher is a probable out. No manager would want to give up two outs to get him to second. The play is to run, which, if successful, gives your eighth-hole hitter a shot. Then your pitcher can force a play by bunting or if allowed to hit he is out of double-play danger.

Eighth Batter

This hitter's biggest job is to bring his pitcher to bat. He must take pitches to allow as much rest as possible to the pitcher. When batting with two out it is most important that he reach base so the pitcher won't have to lead off the next inning. A fair hitter is needed here; in fact, sometimes it is more important to have the better hitter batting eighth position than sixth. One further note: At the youth league level, very often pitchers are among the best athletes on the team and the best batters. Therefore, you would want to bat your pitcher ahead of weaker hitters.

Picking a Coach

Select a good talker who keeps his mind on the game and is able to flash signs with his hands.

Coaching First Base

The coach should never take his eyes off the first baseman on defense with runners on first and second base or with bases full. He should keep the runner infomed at all times. The base-man must not be allowed to slip in and pick him off.

On base hits he should be sure the runner rounds the base. He should advise the runner when to slide into first base, in most cases to avoid a crash or head-on collision with the first base-man.

Coaching Third Base

This is a key position. When waving in a run the coach should come down the line toward home plate. If he decides to stop the runner he should put his hands in his face. If he wants the runner to slide or stand up, he indicates this with his hands and arms.

Often a good coach can wave a runner down on the side of the bag away from the throw, so the runner will know ahead of time which side to take off on.

The coach helps runners tag the base on fly balls. With run-ners on base he must tell the runner ahead of time whether to score or make the ball go through.

Be sure to teach coaches that their first consideration should be the score, next, the inning and third, the number of outs. This helps them decide how to play the game, when to bunt, hit away or steal, and whether to give a run or cut a run off.

basic strategy and tactics
Offense
Hit to Opposite Field

"Go with the pitch" means that the hitter hits a ball thrown on the outside part of the plate to the opposite field; that is, a right-handed hitter would hit the ball to right field and a left-handed hitter would hit to left field.

Hit and Run

The *hit-and-run play* simply means that a runner or runners will break (or run) toward the next base as the pitcher throws to the hitter. The batter has the obligation to hit the ball sharply on the ground if possible, hopefully through the infield position vacated by the fielder leaving his position to cover the base for the steal. It is wise that the hitter be ahead of the pitcher 2-0, or better still, 3-1 to insure that the pitcher throws a strike. Runners should be careful not to get picked off base when the hit and run is on.

Sacrifice Bunt

"Sacrifice bunt" is so called because the hitter sacrifices his chance to hit so as to advance a runner or runners to another base. The bunter squares around or turns his body to face the pitcher when the pitcher takes the ball out of his glove to throw.

Delayed Steal

A *delayed steal* occurs when a baserunner waits or delays until the catcher starts to throw the ball back to the pitcher, then breaks for the next base.

Also, with runners on first and third it means that the runner on first breaks for second to draw the catcher's throw. As the catcher throws, the runner on third breaks for the plate. However, the runner on third must be careful that an infielder does not cut the ball off and return it quickly to the catcher.

Squeeze Plays

There are two types of *squeeze plays:* the safety squeeze and the suicide squeeze. A runner on third breaks for home only at the end of his walking lead off third when the hitter bunts the ball on the ground. This is called a safety squeeze. In the suicide squeeze the runner on third breaks toward home at the moment the pitcher releases the pitch. The batter waits until the pitcher releases the ball before he gives himself up to bunt the ball on the ground. Occasionally there will be runners on second and third when the squeeze is used. The runner on second will try to score while the fielder is trying to throw out the bunter. This play is called the double squeeze.

Sacrifice Fly

A *sacrifice fly* occurs when a runner on third can tag up and score after the ball is caught. The hitter is not credited with a time at bat under such a situation and is credited with a run batted in.

Tag Up and Advance after Catch by Outfielder

A runner may advance at his own risk, of course, after a catch in the outfield. Most often the tag and run is made from second to third or third to home.

A third-base coach should remind the runner on second or third in a situation where there are fewer than two outs to return to the base and run after the catch.

The runner should tag the base with his left foot. He should watch the outfielder himself rather than waiting for a cue from the coach. On deep fly balls, the runner should delay just an instant to make sure the catch has been made. The runner can be called out for leaving the base too soon provided the ball is returned to the base.

Runners should tag up on all flys hit in foul territory. Often in catching the ball, the fielder is carried away from the action giving the runner enough time to advance. However, runners shouldn't tag up on pop-ups within the infield because there isn't time enough to score after the catch. The runner should take a leadoff at a distance which is appropriate to where the ball is being played. If the ball is muffed by the infielder, the runner has less distance to run than if he were still standing on the base.

Defense

Relief Pitching Strategy

Often a left-handed pitcher will be brought in to pitch to a left-handed hitter. This stratagem is used because left-handed hitters usually have more difficulty hitting the curve ball breaking away from them; or it is used to force the offense to use a hitter who bats right. However, this theory doesn't always work. Much depends on the ability and "stuff" a pitcher has rather than whether he is left or right handed.

Pitchout

If the catcher anticipates a stolen base attempt, he should signal the pitcher to throw the ball high and outside the strike zone so that he can best throw to second.

Positioning the Team Defensively

Depending on whether a batter usually hits to left field, right field or straightaway, members of the team on defense should make position adjustments to compensate accordingly.

Alignment of a team on defense for a batter who hits straightaway.

Overshift for Pull Hitters

An overshifted infield defense occurs whenever the infielders move three or four steps from their normal defensive positions such as toward their right (for a right-handed hitter) because the hitter normally "pulls" the ball toward left field.

In cases where a batter is an extremely strong and consistent pull hitter, a manager may choose to position three infielders on one side of the infield leaving only one fielder on the other side.

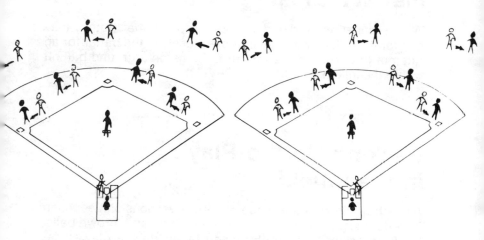

Alignment to compensate for a batter who usually hits to left field.

Defensive positioning for a batter who usually hits to right field.

Fielders usually play deep for power hitters and shallow for weak hitters. Other adjustments may be necessary as the game situation merits.

Defensive Alignment Late in a Close Game

Late in a close game the first and third basemen should play closer to the foul lines, guarding them to prevent possible extra-base hits down the lines. Outfielders should play deeper and the right and left fielders should move toward center (or "bunch").

125

Defensive Alignment of Infield with Two Out and Runners on First and Second

All the infielders should play deeper than normal to prevent a ground ball from getting through. This permits a force-out at any base.

Play at the Plate

With a runner on third and less than two out, the strategy may call for the infielder to play in more closely to the batter for an attempt to throw out the runner at home on a ground ball hit within the infield.

Backing Up the Play in the Infield

Aside from fielding and base coverage responsibilities, each infielder must back up teammates on batted and thrown balls. Back-up positions are determined by where the play is developing.

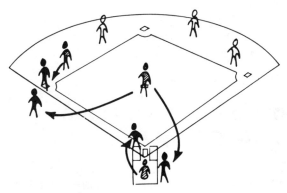

The pitcher backs up the third baseman on throws to third and backs up the catcher on throws to home plate.

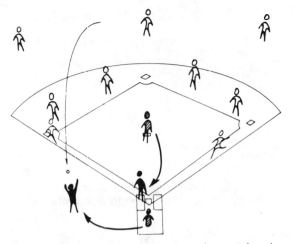

The pitcher covers home when the catcher is drawn away from the plate.

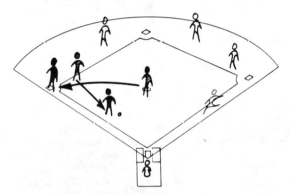

When the third baseman is pulled away from the base as in the case of fielding a bunt, the pitcher covers third base.

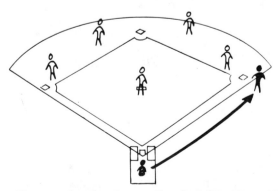

The catcher backs up the first baseman on throws to first base.

The second baseman covers first base when the first baseman is pulled out of position to field a bunt.

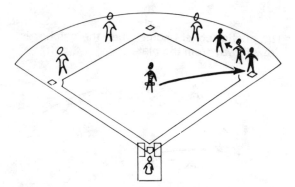

When the first baseman moves to his right to field a ground ball, the pitcher covers first base. *Note that the first baseman may recover in time to tag the base himself. However, on ground balls hit to the first baseman's right, it is always a good practice for the pitcher to break toward first base in case his coverage is necessary.*

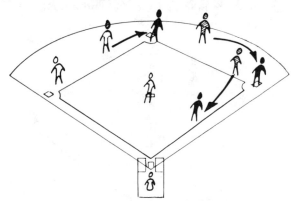

Either the shortstop or the second baseman may cover second base. When the second baseman covers first base, the shortstop is responsible for second base.

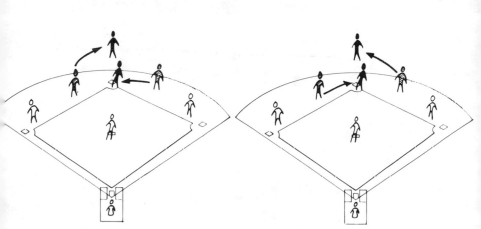

The shortstop backs up the second baseman when the second baseman is covering the base. Conversely, when the shortstop covers the base, the second baseman backs up the play.

Backing Up the Play in the Outfield

Aside from fielding the ball, outfielders also are responsible for backing up infielders on hit or thrown balls as well as for backing up the play of fellow outfielders.

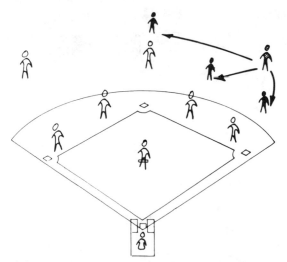

The right fielder backs up the first baseman, second baseman or the center fielder depending on where the play develops.

129

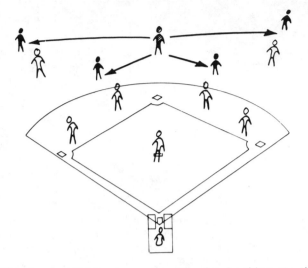

The center fielder is responsible for backing up the right fielder, the left fielder, the second baseman and the shortstop.

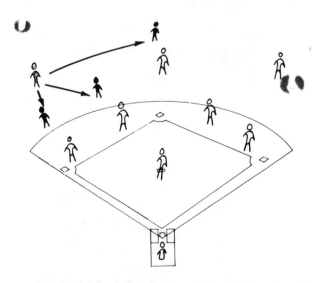

The left fielder backs up the center fielder, the third baseman and the shortstop.

Defensive Situations

Every baseball manager has his own particular interests in the game; my favorite part of baseball is an aggressive, spirited defense. All the defensive plays I teach in youth-league baseball are founded upon four fundamental principles: **Back Up, Cover Up, Talk Up, and Look Up.** The manager who inculcates these principles into his youngsters — and then practices the basic situations set forth in the following diagrams — should be able to expect a strong defense, which will be characterized by good coordination among the players and by the players' knowledge of where to go and whom to throw the ball to. Who has not watched a youth league baseball game and seen players standing by, idle or confused, when they should have to play on almost every ball that is hit? Through teaching and practicing these fundamentals, the manager will impress upon his youngsters that all nine players are actively and cooperatively engaged in defense.

I would suggest that, when the manager first explains these plays, he set the bases thirty feet apart, as is suggested elsewhere in this handbook. Of course, the manager himself must be thoroughly familiar with these plays; he cannot teach what he doesn't understand. After the youngsters have walked through the plays, they should have the opportunity to use them with live runners (who trot or jog along the base paths). When the fielders know their responsibilities, the bases should be restored to their normal intervals. I suggest that the manager first throw the ball, rather than batting it; when the players are familiar with the situations, the manager can hit the ball and introduce live, aggressive base running to test his fielders.

Experienced managers will note that the plays I detail in the situations which are diagrammed here depart from certain established baseball guidelines. For example, in higher-level baseball, the first baseman normally acts as cutoff to the plate (what I call "interior" cutoff) on balls hit to center or right field; and usually the third baseman handles cutoffs to the plate on balls to left field (or at least to the right of the third baseman). If I were managing a college — or probably even a high school — team, that is what I would instruct, too. But, in the youth leagues, I think it's better to have the pitcher serve as interior cutoff. Normally, the pitcher is your best athlete, and he is probably less likely to get "rattled" under the pressure of serving as cutoff. And, because he is already in the center of the diamond, he doesn't have far to go to get into position.

Experienced managers will note, too, that the commands I have fielders use are different from upper-level baseball where, normally, if the receiving baseman says nothing, the throw comes through. I have found that it's best to reinforce the youth leaguers at every step of the play. So I use the command "RELAY" when I want the cutoff man to catch the ball and then continue it to its original base of destination. These commands are, I think, very important; my team practices them quite a bit. I will describe the basic cutoff play, first from the perspective of the receiving baseman (who is the player guarding the base which is the probable base of play), and then I will describe the cutoff man's responsibilities.

Baseman: If the ball is hit into left field (and no one is on base), the second baseman is the baseman (because he is covering the base to which the batter/runner may try to advance). After the ball goes into left field, the baseman commands the shortstop. The shortstop goes into left field, roughly half way (sometimes less) between the fielder picking up or catching the ball and second base. The shortstop should be in a straight line with the batted ball (or the left fielder) and the base of probable play. The shortstop can figure out how far out into the field he should go; but he must depend upon the second baseman for directions, either LEFT or RIGHT, to keep him on line with ball and bag. Therefore, the second baseman issues the directions, loudly. The second baseman will be told by the pitcher and first baseman whether the runner is trying to advance to second. Depending upon the situation the baseman gives one of four commands to the cutoff.

ALL THE WAY: If the second baseman expects a play at the bag and if he knows that the left fielder has a good, reliable arm, the second baseman may command, ALL THE WAY. The baseman then raises both arms in the air, so there is no doubt in the fielder's mind where to throw. The cutoff repeats the command ALL THE WAY, drops his arms, and ducks.

CUT, NO PLAY: If the baseman is advised that the runner has stopped at first and will not be advancing, he commands his cutoff, "CUT, NO PLAY." The shortstop then catches the ball, and runs it back into the infield.

CUT, THREE: Perhaps there will be no play at second, but the baseman sees (assuming there were other runners on base) that there will be a good chance to throw out a runner who's trying for third ("three") or home ("four"). In this case, he commands the cutoff, "CUT, THREE."

RELAY, SECOND: If the runner is trying to get to the base of probable play, the baseman commands, RELAY, SECOND. Thus, there is no doubt in the cutoff man's mind that he must throw the ball and no doubt about where.

Cutoff Man: The cutoff man races to his position about half way between the fielder (and ball) and base of probable play. He follows the directions of his "commander," who is the baseman at the covered bag. The cutoff raises both hands over his head and yells "HERE" to the outfielder. (He would drop his hands only when the baseman shouts ALL THE WAY to the fielder; then the cutoff would repeat the order before ducking down.) As the fielder throws the ball to the cutoff man — who knows what to do with it because of the orders he has received from his baseman — he takes one step toward the ball with his right foot (left foot if he's a southpaw); this will pivot him toward the base to which he is throwing. The cutoff man turns toward his glove — a far shorter and more natural pivot than trying to turn in the opposite direction. He makes his throw about belt-high to the baseman — and fairly hard. Of course, if he hears CUT, NO PLAY, he simply catches the ball and runs it into the center of the diamond.

This play works pretty much the same with an interior cutoff who, in my system, is always the pitcher. The pitcher is governed by the catcher when the base of probable play is home plate. The commands are the same, and the play seems to work well. In the diagrams, you will notice that I try to have every base covered. In case the catcher should command the pitcher to "CUT, TWO" (because perhaps a runner has scored but there may be a play on the batter/runner who is trying for second), there are players in position at every base in case of a rundown. The system of defense I employ results in a number of rundowns (which speaks well of the system, I think). All my players learn the essentials of the rundown, which are: (1) try to run the runner BACK to his base or origin; (2) use a wrist flip, and run with the ball held up, exposed to the fielder at whose base you're forcing the runner; (3) flip the ball to the baseman when he commands NOW; (4) follow the throw to the baseman, getting out of the baseline. A rundown should mean an out; and the out should come with one throw. I teach my first baseman to back up the plate on every rundown in which the plate could be involved.

There is one other play which I think is very important in youth league baseball, and one rarely see it. It is the TANDEM RELAY, so called because the shortstop and the second baseman serve as a two-man (in line) relay team. In case the hitter drives a shot between the outfielders (or if a ball gets by the outfielder), I have the shortstop command, TANDEM. This alerts the second baseman and first baseman to their special duties. On a tandem relay, the shortstop races out to be the lead man on the two-man relay team (this is so because the shortstop normally has the stronger arm). He raises his arms and commands "HERE" — as in a regular cutoff. The second baseman lines up the shortstop between the ball and third base; he stays about ten feet behind the shortstop. The first baseman trails the runner into second, and covers that bag.

The first and third basemen tell the second baseman the status of the runner. The pitcher, meanwhile, serves as interior cutoff (or relay), which can be important on a long throw. For example, on a long shot into right field, the shortstop would race to his position on the tandem, followed by the second baseman. The right or centerfielder would fire the ball to the shortstop, who would in turn throw to third base or home through the pitcher, who is in line with the shortstop and the base of probable play. The importance of the tandem is this: youth leaguers will often overthrow the cutoff man, or they will throw the ball by him on the ground. If a high or low throw escapes the front man on the tandem, the second baseman is there (about ten feet behind) to back it up, thus preventing a home run. It looks more complicated than it is; and I have found that youth leaguers pick up the idea real fast. Teach this play and, if it works only once during a season, it will reward you; the youngsters see their practice pay a nice dividend when some overconfident runner is mowed down at third or home because of the tandem relay.

In the diagrams, the following symbols are used: P=pitcher; C=catcher; 1B=first baseman; 2B=second baseman; 3B=third baseman; SS=shortstop; Of=outfielder (LF, CF, RF=left fielder, center fielder, right fielder); X=the batted ball's destination; R=runner. I have a simple rule for the cutoff situation: Whenever there is a runner on second base and the ball goes into the outfield, the pitcher receives the ball as interior cutoff man. No set of twelve diagrams can make a youth league team; but rehearsal of these situations can result, as the players learn their roles and responsibilities, in demonstrable and dramatic increases in teamwork, confidence, and high spirit. **BACK UP, COVER UP, TALK UP, AND LOOK UP!** Those are the keys to aggressive defense. The players must be taught one other major principle — that when circumstances arise that are not covered by the "book" (that they haven't practiced in situations), they're in charge. The manager teaches the basics, but the players make it happen!

SITUATION ONE: Single to left field, no one on base (or runner on 3rd)

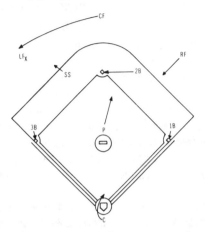

P — moves toward second, and prepares to back up the throw, staying on the infield side and out of the basepath. Talks to 2B about the runner.

C — covers home.

1B — covers first; assists pitcher in telling 2B the status of the runner.

2B — covers second; commands cutoff; gets reports from P and 1B.

SS — goes out to short cutoff spot; follows 2B's orders; prepares to yell "Tandem" if ball eludes LF.

3B — covers third

LF — field ball

CF — races hard to back up LF.

RF — moves into position behind second base in line for possible overthrow; remains on the outfield side and out of the basepath.

Often, in advanced levels of baseball, particular basemen are assigned the job of watching the runner touch the base. I make no such assignments directly, other than generally encouraging my players to watch for that. I do try to instill in the players, particularly the catcher and first baseman, to glance at the bag and to report it quietly to the pitcher before the next pitch (for an appeal) if the runner has missed. I do instruct basemen to watch early leaving on a tag-up.

SITUATION TWO: Ball eludes OF, or long drive past OF.

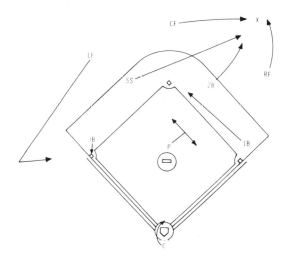

P — prepares to act either as relay man to home or to third (depending upon situation).

C — covers the plate, and helps to line up P with OF and plate, if play at home is in prospect.

1B— watches the runner tag first, and then trails the runner to second, covering second in case of rundown.

2B— when SS commands TANDEM, 2B races to be back man on the tandem relay; listens for status of runner, occasionally glancing back to check; if OF throw to SS is bad, 2B prepares to act as cutoff.

SS— commands TANDEM, and races to be lead element of the relay team.

3B— covers third, and may line up P with third in case of play expected there.

LF— if ball is hit to RF, LF serves as deep back-up at third; if ball is hit to LF or CF, LF makes play or backs up CF.

CF— makes the play or backs up the LF or RF.

RF— if ball is hit to LF, the RF comes in to back up at second in case of possible rundown; if ball is hit to CF or RF, the RF backs up CF or makes the play.

SITUATION THREE: Single to center, no one on base (or man on 3rd)

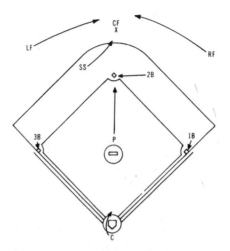

P — backs up throw to second base; talks to 2B.

C — covers home.

1B— covers first, and tells 2B the runner's progress.

2B— covers second, gets reports on runner, commands the cutoff.

SS— serves as cutoff, follows orders from 2B, prepares for Tandem.

3B— covers 3B.

LF— backs up CF.

CF— makes play.

RF— backs up CF.

SITUATION FOUR: Single to right, no one on base (or man on 3rd)

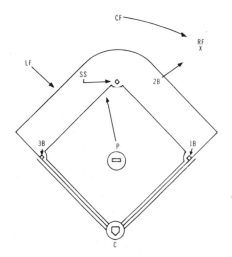

P — backs up shortstop, staying out of the baseline.
C — covers home.
1B— covers first, tells SS about the runner's progress.
2B— goes out to short cutoff position, prepares for tandem if ball gets by the RF a long ways, takes orders from SS.
SS— covers second, prepares to yell TANDEM (if need be)
3B— covers 3B.
LF— serves as deep back-up man on any throw to second.
CF— backs up the RF.
RF— makes the play.

SITUATION FIVE: Single to left, runner on first (or on 1st and 3rd)

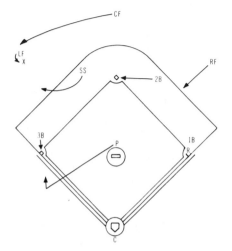

P — backs up third base as deep man.
C — covers home.
1B— covers first.
2B— covers second.
SS— serves as cutoff between third and OF; follows 3B's orders.
3B— covers third, and commands the cutoff.
LF— makes the play.
CF— backs up CF.
RF— races in to back up any possible throw to second base.

SITUATION SIX: Single to centerfield, runner on first (or on 1st and 3rd)

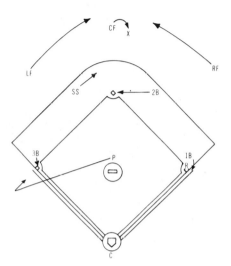

P — serves as deep back-up at third.
C — covers home.
1B — covers first.
2B — covers second.
SS — takes cutoff position in line with CF and 3B; follows 3B's orders.
3B — covers third; commands cutoff.
LF — backs up CF.
CF — makes the play.
RF — backs up CF, but, once the ball is fielded cleanly, moves to back up possible throw to second base.

SITUATION SEVEN: Single to rightfield, runner on first (or 1st and 3rd)

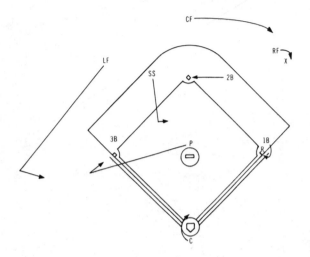

P — serves as close back-up at third base.
C — covers home.
1B— covers first.
2B— covers second.
SS— takes cutoff position in line with RF and 3B; follows 3B's orders.
3B— covers third; command cutoff.
LF— serves as deep back-up at third base.
CF— backs up RF.
RF— makes the play.

SITUATION EIGHT: Single to right or center, runner on second (or on 2nd & 3rd or 1st, 2nd & 3rd)

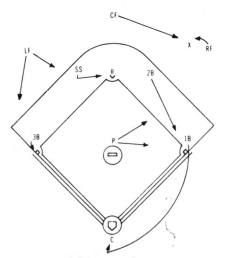

P — acts as interior cutoff, following C's commands. P may have to go out farther into the infield (or even a little into the outfield) to get a good throw from the OF.

C — covers home, commands the cutoff. Be ready to use the command CUT, TWO or CUT, THREE in case there is no play at home but there is one at another base. Be alert!

1B — backs up the plate (note this difference from higher-level baseball). Keep on line with the throw, behind the C. (Covers second if tandem needed)

2B — covers first (unless tandem required)

SS — covers second.

3B — covers third.

LF — backs up possible throw to second; be ready to back up third base, too.

CF — backs up or fields ball.

RF — backs up or fields ball.

NOTE: The CF is the primary OF, and has priority on all fly balls. OF calls for ball by saying twice (if there is time), "I've got it; I've got it." Fielders near him yell, "Take it, Bobby; take it, Bobby" (using player's first name). On all pop-ups behind the infielders, they are to go back and try to make the play until called off by the OF, who should call off the infielder if possible (because it's easier for the incoming OF to make the catch).

Back Up, Cover Up, Talk Up, Look Up — after every play!

SITUATION NINE: Single to left field, runner on second (or on 2nd
and 3rd, or on 1st, 2nd, and 3rd)

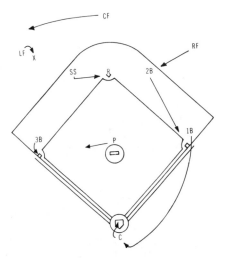

P — serves as interior cutoff man.
C — commands the interior cutoff.
1B— backs up the C.
2B— covers first, except in case of tandem relay.
SS— covers second.
3B— covers third.
LF— makes the play.
CF— backs up LF.
RF— backs up possible throw to second.

This situation is about the same with a single to RIGHT with a
runner on second (or 3rd and 2nd, or on 1st, 2nd, and 3rd), except that the P would line up home and RF, guided by the C; the
1B would back up home on the third base side of the diamond;
the LF would back up third base; and the RF would make the play,
backed up by a racing CF.

SITUATION TEN: Single to center with runner on second (or on 2nd and 3rd, or on 1st, 2nd, and 3rd)

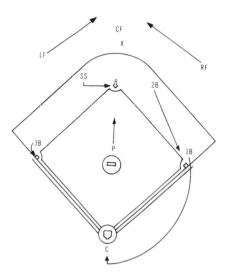

P — serves as interior cutoff man.
C — covers home, and commands the cutoff.
1B — backs up the C.
2B — covers first.
SS — covers second.
3B — covers third.
LF — backs up CF.
CF — makes thc play.
RF — backs up CF.

NOTE: The CF's throw is not to the SS, but to the P, who has both hands raised over his head and is yelling "HERE." If a runner is trapped, say between second and third (and this can often happen when the ball is thrown to the interior cutoff man), the P would RUN HARD AT THE RUNNER, forcing him into the rundown. Many youth leaguers will freeze when the fielder runs hard at them, permitting the charging fielder to tag the hapless runner, and then to LOOK UP for another possibly play. Keep emphasizing the principles: BACK UP, COVER UP, TALK UP, LOOK UP.

SITUATION ELEVEN: Basic bunt defense (with no one on base)

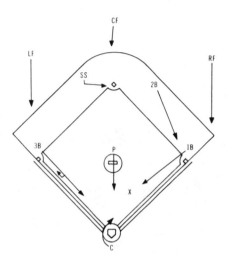

P — charges straight ahead, watching out for the fake bunt or "slash hit."

C — commands the play, flipping off the mask, and charging out from behind the plate. Remember: all four bases are in FAIR territory.

1B— yells "BUNT" (to jar the defense into action) and charges.

2B— races to first base.

SS— covers second base.

3B— also yells "BUNT" and charges; quickly returns to third if he doesn't handle the ball.

LF — backs up third.

CF— backs up second.

RF— backs up first; get there quickly!

If there is a runner on first base: The play is about the same as the play above. The P and 3B must TALK UP so that one of them covers third. An alert runner on first may try to get to third if he sees it left unguarded. The outfielders should be on line with the probable throw in backing up. Do not leave a base unguarded: BACK UP, COVER UP, TALK UP, LOOK UP!

SITUATION TWELVE: Bunt defense (with runners on first and second)

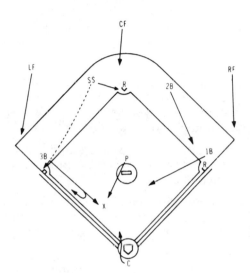

P — charges, favoring his right side.
C — commands the play, and may pop out to make the play.
1B — yells "BUNT," and charges.
2B — races to cover first.
SS — covers second — UNLESS he receives a signal from the manager (I use the verbal command "TIGHT DEFENSE, TIGHT DEFENSE") that he should cover third in an effort to get the lead runner.
3B — yells "BUNT" and charges.
LF — backs up third.
RF — backs up first.
CF — backs up second, and prepares to COVER SECOND if he hears or sees the signal meaning that the SS will be covering third.

The bunt defense with the bases loaded works pretty much the same, except the play (if possible) will be to the plate. The C has only to step on the plate, because it's a force play. It is very possible for the C to take a toss from the charging 3B, P, or 1B, and then throw to the 2B at first to get a double play. LOOK UP AFTER EVERY PLAY. If you can't get the lead runner on the bunt, then be sure to take the out.

rules simplified

Today's baseball is a very different ball than the rubber ball used years ago. Now, the ball is constructed with a cork or rubber center, a tight wool winding and a horsehide cover.

Each player is required to wear a mitt (glove), the type of which is prescribed by rules of the game relative to the position played. For instance, a player cannot wear a first baseman's glove ("trapper model") when playing in the outfield.

Bats are scientifically designed and standardized in various sizes to accommodate the physical attributes and personal preferences of all ball players.

The standard baseball diamond is 90 feet on each side (90 feet between bases). Lines extend straight out from home plate beyond first and third base to separate fair from foul territory.

The batter's box on either side of home plate is four feet by six feet. Home plate itself is 17 inches wide and 17 inches from the front to the back corner. (See Page 83 for typical youth league diamond dimensions.)

The pitcher and catcher as a pair are known as the battery. The distance from the front of the pitcher's plate to the back corner of home plate is 60 feet, six inches.

The first baseman, the second baseman, the shortstop and the third baseman are known as infielders. Completing the nine-man team and known as the outfielders are the right fielder, the center fielder and the left fielder.

A game is divided into nine innings. Each team is allowed one turn at bat per inning. With the third out, a team's turn at bat ends. That team then takes the field and the opposing team bats. Rules provide that a game be as many as nine innings long. Specific youth league rules may provide that a game be shorter.

The team with the greatest number of runs at the end of nine innings is the winner. A run is scored when a runner touches home plate preceded by tagging first, second and third bases. Extra innings are played to determine the winner of a game tied after the end of regulation play. An official game may be recorded after five innings (after 4½ innings if the home team is leading) should rain or inclement weather cause play to be suspended.

Dimensions
Standard Baseball Diamond

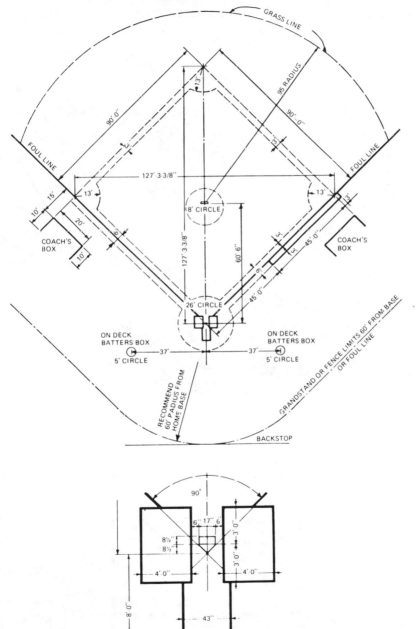

Dimensions
Typical Youth League Diamond

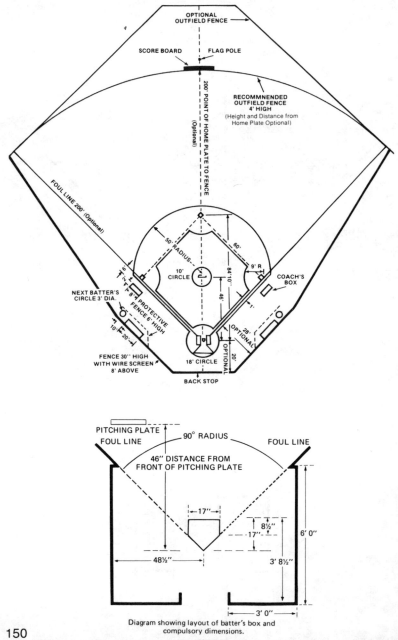

Diagram showing layout of batter's box and
compulsory dimensions.

Learn to Keep Score

The ability to keep an accurate record of the play-by-play action of a baseball game adds much to the enjoyment of watching and playing the game. Keeping score is easily done by using numbers and abbreviations to identify the players and their actions during the game. These are numbers and abbreviations which are commonly used:

POSITION NUMBERS OF PLAYERS

1—Pitcher	4—2nd Baseman	7—Left Fielder
2—Catcher	5—3rd Baseman	8—Center Fielder
3—1st Baseman	6—Shortstop	9—Right Fielder

ACTION DURING PLAY

W	—Walk	PB	—Passed Ball	AB	—Times at Bat
K	—Strike Out	WP	—Wild Pitch	R	—Runs
E	—Error	HP	—Hit by Pitch	H	—Hits
B	—Balk	DP	—Double Play	RBI	—Runs Batted In
O	—Out	TP	—Triple Play	G	—Ground Ball
F	—Foul Out	S	—Stolen Base		(for unassisted
FO	—Force-Out	OS	—Out Stealing		infield outs)
H	—Sacrifice	FC	—Fielder's Choice		

On the following pages is a record of the play of one team during an imaginary nine-inning game. Compare the play-by-play account of this game (Pages 86 and 87) with the scorecard of the same game to learn scorekeeping techniques.

You will notice on the scorecard that the batter's progress around the bases is indicated by diagonal lines within his own inning-square. Each line represents one base marked in a clockwise direction. Above each line is a small letter or number which explains how the batter or runner moved to that particular base, or in the case of a batter making a hit, to what field the ball travelled. Succeeding numbers then show either the number of the teammate who moved him to the next base or bases, or the letter describing another reason for his advance.

For instance, the first batter in the sixth inning, Cox, got to first base on a single (one diagonal line) to center field (8). He stole second base (S). He went to third on what Mitchell (9) did. Extra-base hits are indicated by diagonal lines equal to the number of bases made. For example, the first batter in the seventh inning hit a home run, shown by four lines to all four bases. In the third inning, Jones got a double shown by two lines to second base.

SCORECARD

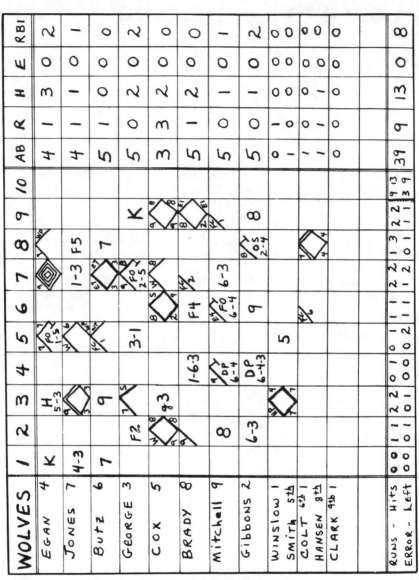

The Play-By-Play

First Inning: Egan (2b) struck out. Jones (lf) grounded out, second baseman to first. Butz (ss) flied out to left field.

Second Inning: George (1b) fouled out to the catcher. Cox (3b) walked. Brady (cf) singled to right field, sending Cox to third base. Mitchell (rf) flied out to center, Cox scoring after the catch. Gibbons (c) grounded out, shortstop to first.

Third Inning: Winslow (p) was hit by a pitched ball and took first base. Egan sacrificed Winslow to second, and was thrown out, third baseman to first. Jones doubled to right field, scoring Winslow from second. Butz flied out to right field. George singled to left, scoring Jones from second. George stole second base. Cox grounded out to the first baseman, unassisted.

Fourth Inning: Brady grounded out, shortstop to first after the pitcher deflected the ball for an assist. Mitchell singled to right. Gibbons hit into a double play, shortstop to second base to first. Mitchell was forced at second.

Fifth Inning: Smith batted for the pitcher Winslow and lined out to the third baseman. Egan singled to left, Jones walked, moving Egan to second. Butz was safe on a fielder's choice when the pitcher took his grounder and threw to the third baseman for a force-out on Egan, Jones taking second on the play. Jones and Butz advanced to third and second on a wild pitch. George grounded to the first baseman who threw to the pitcher covering first base for the third out. Colt came in to pitch.

Sixth Inning: Cox singled to center. Brady fouled out to the second baseman. Cox stole second base. Mitchell was safe on an error by the second baseman, Cox taking third on the play. Gibbons flied out to right, Cox scoring from third after the catch. Colt grounded to the shortstop, who elected to throw to the second baseman for a force-out on Mitchell to retire the side.

Seventh Inning: Egan hit a home run over the right-field fence. Jones grounded out, pitcher to first. Butz went all the way to second base when the left fielder dropped his fly ball. George singled to right, scoring Butz. George went to second on a balk. Cox walked. Brady was safe on a fielder's choice when the catcher took his short grounder and threw to the third baseman for a force-out on George. Mitchell rolled out, shortstop to first.

Eighth Inning: Gibbons singled to center. Gibbons tried to steal second and was thrown out, catcher to second baseman. Hansen batted for the pitcher Colt and doubled to left. Egan singled to right, scoring Hansen from second. Egan took second on a wild pitch. Jones fouled out to the third baseman. Butz flied out to left.

Ninth Inning: George struck out. Cox singled to right. Brady singled to center, Cox taking third. Mitchell was safe on a fielder's choice when the pitcher took his grounder and, trying for a double play, threw wildly to second base, Cox scoring on the error and Brady going all the way to third. Gibbons flied to center, Brady scoring after the catch. (In this example, this last run broke a tie game in the last of the ninth, so the game is immediately over, the Wolves winning 9 to 8.)

glossary of baseball terms

ABOARD: A player on base is said to be "aboard."

ARBITER: An umpire.

ASSIST: A fielding credit earned by a player who helps a teammate make a put-out. Should the teammate fail to make the put-out because of a misplay, the first player is still given credit for an assist.

AWAY: The number of outs, such as "one away" instead of "one out."

BACKSTOP: While a catcher is often called "the backstop," the term is more often applied to the fencing behind the plate.

BACK UP: To take a position to the rear of a teammate to retrieve any balls which the teammate might fail to catch.

BAG: A base. Also called "sack," "hassock," "pillow," "canvas," etc.

BALK: Making a motion to pitch without immediately delivering the ball to the batter.

BALL: Today's baseball is composed of a cork or rubber center with a tight wool winding and horsehide cover. Check league rules regarding size and weight requirements.

"BALL": The term applied to a pitched ball which does not enter the batter's strike zone, and which the batter does not attempt to hit with his bat. (See "Base on Balls.")

BASE: The four "stations" on a ballfield which runners on the offensive team must touch in succession before scoring — first base, second base, third base and home base known as home plate.

BASE HIT: A batted ball which allows the batter to reach a base safely, provided that he does not reach first base through a fielding error or a fielder's choice and provided that no other runner is forced out.

BASE LINE: A more-or-less imaginary space, six feet wide, within which a runner must stay while running bases. If the runner flagrantly moves outside of this lane, he can be called out unless he is trying to avoid a fielder who is attempting to catch a batted ball.

BASE ON BALLS: The penalty imposed on a pitcher who delivers four "balls" to a batter. The batter is allowed to go to first base.

BASES FULL: Baserunners on first, second and third base. Also known as "bases loaded," "bases jammed," "three men on," etc.

BAT: A regulation baseball bat must be of one-piece wood or approved material. Bats are constructed in a variety of lengths and weights. Check your league rules for size and weight requirements.

BATTER'S BOX: The area in which the batter must stand. There is a batter's box on each side of home plate. Each is six feet long and four feet wide, and is placed six inches from home plate.

BATTERY: The combination of the pitcher and the catcher.

BATTING AVERAGE: The number of hits divided by the number of times at bat. The result is usually expressed in three decimals.

BATTING ORDER: The order in which players take their turn at bat. It is set before the game begins, and cannot be changed during play. However, player substitutes can be made.

BEAT OUT: To hit a ball to an infielder and reach first base ahead of that fielder's throw, for a hit.

BLEEDER: A batted ball which just trickles past the defensive players for a "weak" base hit.

BLOOPER: A batted ball which arches over the heads of the infielders and drops in front of the outfielders for a base hit.

BOBBLE: Juggling the ball while attempting a catch, or dropping the ball for an error.

BOTTOM: The second part of an inning. For instance, the second half of the fourth inning is known as the "bottom" of the fourth. The first part of an inning is known as the "top."

BOX SCORE: A description of the events of a game kept in condensed form by the use of certain symbols for the various types of possible plays.

BUNT: A ball tapped by a batter to roll slowly out into the infield. Bunts are usually attempted in an effort to advance another baserunner, but they are also used to allow the batter to reach first base safely by catching the defensive team off guard.

CATCHER: The defensive player who stands behind home plate to receive balls thrown by the pitcher.

CENTER FIELDER: The defensive player who guards center field, the outfield area beyond second base.

CHANGE-OF-PACE: A pitcher's ability to vary the speed of his delivery of pitches, thus confusing the batter.

CHEST PROTECTOR: A device used by a catcher or a plate umpire to keep hard-thrown or hard-hit balls from causing injury.

CHOKE: To grip a baseball bat more closely to the "trademark" than is usual. "Choking the bat" is often done to gain accuracy in hitting the ball.

CIRCUIT CLOUT: A home run. Batter circles all four bases.

CLEAN THE BASES: To hit a home run with players on base, thus clearing all the bases of runners.

CLEAN-UP: The fourth position in the batting order, usually given to the best hitter on the team on the theory that he will drive in more runs.

COACH: A member of the team who stands near either first or third base to give baserunning instructions to the team's players.

COMPLIMENTARY RUNNER: A substitute baserunner, who by mutual consent of the opposing coaches or managers does not prevent the original runner from remaining in the game.

CORNER: Portions of home plate; the part of the plate closest to a batter is known as "the inside corner." The part farthest from him is known as "the outside corner." The other bases are known as "the initial corner" (first base), the "keystone corner" (second base), and the "hot corner" (third base).

COUNT: The number of balls and strikes on a batter. A count of "1 and 2" means that the batter has one ball and two strikes on him.

COUNTER: A run. Also "tally," "marker."

CROWDING THE PLATE: A batter moving close to the plate and refusing to back away with the pitch.

CURVE: A ball pitched with spin to move in a curve rather than a straight path.

CUT: To swing at a pitched ball. Also, a ball which passes over a corner of home plate is said to "cut the corner" for a strike.

CUT-OFF: To intercept a ball thrown to another teammate. A fielder will often cut off a throw aimed at home plate to trap a player running to another base.

DEAD BALL: A ball no longer in play.

DEEP: A defensive player who stands some distance beyond his usual playing position is said to be playing "deep." Opposite of "shallow."

DELAYED STEAL: An attempt to steal a base whereby the runner does not start his dash until the usual moment for attempting the steal has passed. (See Steal).

DELIVER: To pitch the ball.

DIAMOND: The area formed by the four bases.

DIE: To be stranded on a base as the third out is made.

DOUBLE: A base hit on which the batter is able to reach second base safely despite errorless fielding by the defensive team.

DOUBLE PLAY: Two consecutive put-outs made between the time the pitcher delivered the ball to the batter and the time the ball is returned to him again in the pitcher's box. Also called "twin-killing."

DOUBLE STEAL: A "double steal" occurs when two runners steal bases on the same play.

DOWN: Denotes outs. "Two Down" means that there are two outs.

DRIVE: A hard-hit ball which travels in a fairly straight line.

DROP: A type of pitch in which the ball drops downward as it nears or crosses the plate.

EARNED RUN: A run which was scored through offensive play rather than through a defensive error.

EARNED RUN AVERAGE: The average number of earned runs which a pitcher allows during a full game. To find the earned run average, divide the number of earned runs allowed by the number of innings pitched and multiply by nine.

ERROR: Any defensive misplay which allows a batter to remain at bat longer than he should, or a baserunner to remain on base longer than he should, or a runner to reach base or take an extra base. However, a base on balls is not an error, nor is a wild pitch or a passed ball.

EXTRA-BASE HIT: A base hit on which the batter gets more than one base.

FAIR BALL: Any legally batted ball which is touched or which stops in fair territory between home plate and first base or home plate and third base; or which lands inside either foul line when bouncing past first or third base; or which first hits on or inside either foul line on a fly past the infield.

FIELDER'S CHOICE: A play in which a fielder, after taking a batted ball, elects to make a play on a baserunner rather than on the batter.

FIELDING AVERAGE: To find a fielder's defensive average, add his total fielding chances (put-outs, assists and errors) and divide this number into the total of his put-outs and assists.

FIRST BASE: The base to which the batter runs after hitting the ball. It is 90 feet from home plate, along the right-field foul line.

FIRST BASEMAN: The defensive player who covers the territory around first base and who generally retires a large number of batters by receiving the throws of the other infielders after the batter has hit a ground ball.

FLY: A ball that is hit into the air, usually to the outfield.

FORCE-OUT: An out occurring when a defensive player in possession of the ball touches any base before a runner who *must* reach that base touches the base. Thus, the ordinary out at first base is a force-out. However, the term is usually applied to situations in which there are runners on base before the batter hits the ball. Force-outs can occur at any of the four bases.

FORFEIT: An umpire may forfeit any game and award it to one team for a variety of reasons, such as delay of game, refusal to continue play, rule violations, etc. The score of a forfeited game is 9-0 in favor of the team not at fault.

FOUL BALL: A batted ball which is touched or stops outside of the foul line between home plate and first or third base; which bounces past first or third base in foul territory; or which first lands outside the foul lines on a fly ball past first or third base. A foul caught on the fly is an out for the batter. The first two foul hits in a time at bat count as strikes; succeeding ones do not. However, a foul bunt attempt after two strikes is an out for the batter.

FOUL LINE: A three-inch white line extending from home plate out to the boundaries of the playing field. The two foul lines form right angles at home plate. The foul line itself is considered fair territory.

FOUL TIP: A foul ball caught by the catcher immediately after leaving the hitter's bat on a direct line into the catcher's hands. Any foul tip is a strike and the ball remains in play.

FULL COUNT: A count of three balls and two strikes on the batter.

FUNGO: A high fly, usually hit by tossing the ball from the hand and then hitting it, to give the fielders practice.

GAME: A game consists of nine innings. The team which has scored the most runs at the end of that time wins the game, unless tied, in which case the game goes into extra innings. If the team batting in the bottom half of each inning scores more runs in eight than the team batting in the top half of the inning scores in nine turns at bat, the game ends without having to play the last half of the ninth inning.

GRAND SLAM: A home run with the bases loaded.

GRASS CUTTER: A sharply hit ball which skims across the top of the grass.

GROOVE: To pitch the ball right in the middle of the strike zone.

GROUNDER: A "grounder" or "ground ball" is a batted ball which hits the ground as soon as it leaves the player's bat and bounces in the infield as it moves toward the outfield.

HIGH: A pitched ball which passes the plate above the strike zone.

HIT: To take one's turn at bat. Also, to make a base hit.

HIT-AND-RUN: An offensive play in which a baserunner begins running as soon as the pitcher starts his delivery. The batter then attempts to hit the ball, often through a spot vacated by the shortstop or second baseman. Often used as a device for avoiding double plays.

HIT BATSMAN: A batter who is hit by a pitched ball. The batter is entitled to move to first base. However, he must make an attempt to get out of the path of the ball.

HIT THE DIRT: To slide.

HOLE: An area not covered by a defensive player. Fielders often shift positions against certain batters, leaving large "holes" open which normally don't exist.

HOMER: Short for "Home Run." A base hit whereby the batter runs all the bases and scores a run. Most home runs result from balls hit over the outfield fences. Some result from fast baserunning following a ball hit well out of outfielders' reach, but within the playing area.

HOOK SLIDE: A baserunning maneuver in which the runner, trying to reach a base on a close play, slides feet first into the base and twists his body away from the defensive player to touch the base with his rear foot.

INFIELD: Generally, that fair territory bounded by and including the basepaths.

INFIELD HIT: A base hit which does not go past the infielders to the outfield.

INNING: A division of a game. An inning is divided into two halves. A team is allowed to bat during one half of each inning. Since each team is allowed three outs, there are six outs per inning.

INSIDE: A pitch which misses the plate on the side closest to the batter.

LAY ONE DOWN: To bunt the ball.

LEAD: A baserunner "takes a lead" when he moves off a base in an effort to put himself closer to the next base. His "lead" cannot be too great, or he may be tagged out.

LEADOFF: The player who first bats for his team either in the regular batting order or at the beginning of an inning.

LEFT FIELDER: The defensive player who covers the outfield area beyond third base and shortstop.

LINE DRIVE: A ball batted sharply to travel in a fairly straight line. Also a "clothesliner."

LOSING PITCHER: The pitcher who is charged with the loss if his team is defeated.

MASK: A device worn by catchers and umpires to protect their faces against injury from a batted or thrown ball.

MIX UP: To vary the type and speed of pitches.

MOVE UP: To advance to the next base.

MUFF: To drop a ball.

NO-HITTER: A game in which the pitcher does not give up a single hit, and usually no runs. A "perfect game" is one in which no opponent reaches first base on a hit, error, walk, etc.

ONE-TWO-THREE: Side retired without a batter reaching first base.

OUT: An "out" is the retirement of a batter or baserunner during play. The ways in which a batter or baserunner may be put out are numerous. Each team is allowed three outs during its time at bat in any one inning.

OUTFIELD: In general, the fair territory beyond the infield.

OUTSIDE: A pitched ball which misses the strike zone on the side of the plate farthest from the batter.

OVERRUN: To run past a base or to slide past (overslide) a base placing the runner in danger of being tagged out. However, the batter may overrun first base while attempting to reach it after hitting the ball.

PASSED BALL: A legally pitched ball which the catcher fails to hold and control provided that the bat did not strike the ball.

PICK OFF: To trap a runner off base with a sudden throw and tag him out.

PINCH HITTER: A player who is sent into the game to bat in place of another player.

PITCHER'S BOX: The place from which the pitcher delivers the ball. In the pitcher's box is the "rubber" or pitcher's plate, a rubber or wood block set flush with the ground. This "rubber" is 60'6" from the far corner of home plate.

PITCHOUT: A pitch purposely thrown wide of the plate to allow the catcher easier access to the ball. Used to stop a possible steal or hit-and-run.

POP-UP: A short, high fly in or near the infield which can be easily caught.

PUT-OUT: The retiring of a batter or baserunner.

RELAY: To return the ball from the outfield to the infield by using several short, fast throws rather than one long (and necessarily slower) throw. For most relays, an infielder moves out into the outfield, takes the throw from the outfielder, and in turn throws it to another infielder.

RIGHT FIELDER: The defensive player who covers the outfield area beyond first base and second base.

RUN: A unit of scoring. A run is scored when a runner touches home plate, having previously touched first, second and third bases. The run is counted provided the runner is not forced out, tagged out or the batter is retired for the third out of the inning.

RUNS BATTED IN (RBI): A batter is credited with batting in a run when a baserunner scores when he makes a base hit, a sacrifice, forces in a run by walking or hits into a put-out.

SACRIFICE: An advancement of a baserunner by the batter who deliberately hits the ball in such a way that the defensive fielders can only make a play on the batter.

SCRATCH HIT: A ball, usually weakly hit, which none of the fielders can reach in time to retire the batter.

SECOND BASE: The next base after first base. It is the only base not touching the foul lines.

SECOND BASEMAN: The defensive player who generally covers second base and the area to the first base side of second.

SHORTSTOP: A defensive player who generally covers second base and the area to the third base side of second.

SHUT OUT: To prevent the opposing team from scoring a run.

SINGLE: A base hit on which the batter reaches and stops on first base.

SLIDE: Sliding along the ground toward the base to avoid being put out.

SQUEEZE: Advancing a runner from third to home plate by bunting the ball. The baserunner starts running as soon as the ball is pitched. If the batter hits the ball properly, the defensive team has very little time to retire the runner.

STEAL: To advance to another base on the strength of baserunning alone. A runner may steal any base but first.

STRAIGHTAWAY: The term used to describe the normal defensive position of a team, wherein each player remains in his usual fielding area rather than shifting to the right or left.

STRIKE: A penalty imposed on the batter for either failing to hit a ball which enters the strike zone; swinging at any pitch and missing it; or hitting a foul ball which is not caught on the fly. In the latter case, if two strikes are on the batter, a foul ball does not count as another strike. If a batter with two strikes bunts a foul ball, he is out. The strike zone is ordinarily described as that area bounded by the sides of home plate and the batter's shoulders and knees.

TAG UP: The action of a baserunner in touching a base while a fielder is catching a fly ball. The runner must do so if he desires to advance to the next base without danger of being put out at the base from which he leaves. If he leaves this base before a fielder catches the ball, he can be put out providing a defensive player touches this base with the ball in his possession before the runner returns to tag the base.

TEXAS LEAGUER: A weakly-hit fly ball which arches over the heads of the infielders and drops in front of the outfielders for a base hit.

THIRD BASE: The next base after second base. Its outside edge touches the left field foul line. Next stop—home plate!

THIRD BASEMAN: The defensive player who covers the area around third base.

TOP: To hit the top portion of the ball so that the ball bounces downward sharply, resulting in a weak ground ball.

TRAP: To catch a ball immediately after it has taken its first bounce.

TRIPLE: To make a three-base hit.

TRIPLE PLAY: The retirement of three offensive players between the time a ball leaves the pitcher's hand and is returned to him in the pitcher's box. It can only occur with at least two runners on base and no one out, hence is rare.

WAIT OUT: An offensive strategy by a batter who refuses to swing at the pitcher's throws until he either gets a base hit or makes the pitcher throw a good ball to hit.

WALK: A base on balls. Also called a "pass," a "free ticket," a "gift," etc.

WILD PITCH: An inaccurately delivered pitch which the catcher has little or no chance of stopping or holding. It is not counted as such unless the throw permits the batter to reach first base or a baserunner advances.